FULL CIRCLE

FULL CIRCLE

ALVIN "SURREAL" SURRENCY

Library of Congress Control Number: 2019907603
ISBN: Hardcover   978-1-7960-4024-1
                 Softcover   978-1-7960-4025-8
                 eBook   978-1-7960-4037-1

Print information available on the last page.

Rev. date: 06/12/2019

To order additional copies of this book, contact:
Xlibris
1-888-795-4274
www.Xlibris.com
Orders@Xlibris.com
795779

FULL CIRCLE

ALVIN "SURREAL" SURRENCY

Library of Congress Control Number:		2019907603
ISBN:	Hardcover	978-1-7960-4024-1
	Softcover	978-1-7960-4025-8
	eBook	978-1-7960-4037-1

Print information available on the last page.

Rev. date: 06/12/2019

To order additional copies of this book, contact:
Xlibris
1-888-795-4274
www.Xlibris.com
Orders@Xlibris.com
795779

CONTENTS

270° INSPIRATION
♎

360° REAL TALK
♑

365° VAYEB
X

DEDICATION

This entire book is dedicated to a great man. The world knew him as Leonard Surrency. Some knew him as Catfram. I knew him as Dad. I wish that he was here to witness his son publishing his own book. Not just a book, but a book full of poems that salivate attitude, swag, and also wisdom. This is dedicated to him because all of those things I mentioned. I get them all from him. If you know me, then you know him and vice versa. I am truly my father's child.

I always do my best to make you proud and also add on good aspects to our legacy. I thank you for my ways and also my life. I miss you, and I will always love you. See you on the other side.

ACKNOWLEDGMENTS

I would first and foremost thank the Most High for life and all of everything that has been stored for me. I thank the universe and my ancestors, for without them, there is no me. I can't thank my mom, Alma Surrency, enough. She and her prayers have always been in my corner on everything I do. My dad, Leonard Surrency, I'm thankful for having his stubborn but aggressive and temperamental ways. Had I not had his qualities, none of this could have ever happened. I'll always be grateful to my brother, Tyrone Surrency simply because he's the one who initially set a fire under my ass to make this happen. Chantrae Cottingham, Anitra Jackson, and Gee Remarkable, I can't thank you guys enough. You all had a big part in what I've been able to do. Chantrae stayed sharing my work, getting it out to the public. Anitra stayed on me to master my craft and introduced me to an awesome partner. Gee, I appreciate all the assistance you've given me with your camera. I won't ever forget you. Also, I'd like to thank Sergeant Whitaker. Because of his style of leadership, I wrote my very first poem; thank you for being an ass. There are many others who I really do appreciate, no disrespect to anyone but, I had to mention the key players involved. Your assistance, words of encouragement, acting, prayers, accolades has been warmly received and most definitely appreciated.

INTRODUCTION

This book contains poems that have been written over the course of some twenty years. Everything written has some personal dealings behind it, so there's nothing fake about them. Everything you read will be straight up with no chase nor ice.

The first set of poems deals with all the dealings of being black in Amerikkka. These are all things that I've gone through and also bore witness to. This definitely isn't an area to take lightly. Although it is 2019, the same crap is still very much alive. You don't have to take my word for it. I know you have eyes yourself.

In the second set, many of you will take these poems as controversial. Remember, when a mass of people are all on the same mind-set, of course something different is going to make you uncomfortable. Again, I'm only writing the things that I've gone through or currently going through. This is the section where I advise you to seriously research for yourself and fact-check me, if you please.

The third installation of poems is something that we all can use in our lives. Inspiration comes in many forms, whether it be from religion, family, book, etcetera. I've put my personal dealings in here, whether good or bad. You will see that I've had my own share of some strongholds, also that I do acknowledge them and try to correct it. I hope my pain can help ease yours.

The fourth set of poems is where I let everything go and everything out. This area is where I needed to vent and was pushed to the limit and much anger. This area is not for the weak. This is where I put out what I was given. There were many who inspired these, of course in the wrong way and this is my response.

Lastly, the fifth set of poems is notably my creative side. These are aspects in my life that were good, and my mind went wondering. A few tells a little bit about my life and past. Also, there are two in there which I must admit had hypothetical scenarios that ran through my mind.

I do hope that you enjoy my works that I have put together. I did this in order to get my craft out to the world, gain feedback, and more so, leave something behind in this world. Peace, love, and abundance to all.

A LITTLE WHITE LIE

A little white lie, what a whole bunch of bullshit
This everyday choice of words has gotten on my nerves and has made me sick

Where in the hell did this sickening phrase ever come from?
It's so damn insulting, so ignorant, and so very dumb

How did color ever come into place to differentiate the kinds of a lie?
And how did the color white become small and innocent?
I really wanna know why

If we're gonna use color, let's be totally honest and let's tell the truth
If you look at the history and current events of white people, there lies the proof

There's nothing small and innocent about the old
and current status of the white race
Countless acts of lynching, murders, scandals, lies, torture,
takeovers, and plain evil have taken place
Don't take my word for it
It's all in history books
It can also be seen in the news every day
For those of you who disagree and constantly make excuses,
it's totally obvious the direction you sway

Someone once used the expression "If it's white, then it's all right"

There's no measuring a lie
A lie is a lie, always wrong and never right

We've all been hoodwinked, bamboozled, led into
yet another slice of the American pie
Accepting and excusing what really is the biggest
lie better known as the little white lie

1

A NIGHTMARE ON MY RACE

Lie down and get comfortable
Close your eyes
I got a story I wanna tell
In all due fairness, this story is demented, fucked up, and gory as hell

There once was a land, vast and rich, filled with tribes
of black people living their progressive life
Going on with their daily routines, having not a single worry or strife

Then out of nowhere, a gang of pale-faced people
dropped in and not for a cup of tea
In their eyes, this rich land was full of commodities as far as the eye can see
With absolute no regard to human life, the tribesmen were
suddenly chained, counted, and locked up on a boat
This was the initial start of a new way of life, a
culture interrupted, erased, and invoked

Over the course of some four hundred years, millions of tribesmen
would be stolen, transported, and turned into slaves
About another million wouldn't finish the two-thousand-mile
journey, dying and being tossed in the sea of waves

Boatloads filled with hundreds of tribesmen, all chained and laid
on their backs, having to deal with such harsh conditions
The necessity of water, a balanced meal, sanitary bathroom
facilities, medical aid, all these things were never given

These tribesmen arrived in a foreign land to be introduced
to their master and their new home
Families immediately broken up and separated around
foreign people and tribes, feeling all alone

Forced to endure countless hours of work and labor,
being looked at and used as mules
Dreadful means of discipline was used to ensure the
slave mind-set was implemented and infused

With the use of a bullwhip, torn flesh be ripped away from their backs
Even with the thought or idea if the tribesmen
reading was enough to initiate an attack
Hot pokers inserted inside a woman's vagina, testicles
sliced away, and feet chopped off
These were the results of sassing the master or running off

Men savagely beaten damn near to death in front of his family, striking
fear in the hearts of all slaves, a platform created for all slaves to see

Children sold off to other plantations no matter how
much they screamed and tried to fight
That same grieving mother who lost her children taken
advantage of and raped that very same night

With all the terror that was done to the tribesmen, it was
easy to have them do as they bid and submit
Scare and terror tactics shared to all slave owners by a man named Willie Lynch

After a few hundred years of slavery, the emancipation
proclamation was installed by Abraham Lincoln
It initially freed the slaves, but truth be told, all that did was change the slave season
By this time, their entire culture was literally erased, given
a slave name and also a new God and religion
Their mind was not their own, having to accept and never question all that was given

Forced to fend for themselves, poor, illiterate, and ignorant
like a mouse in a room full of hungry cats
Having to watch the paleface live like kings and queens,
reaping the fruits of the work from their backs

Some were able to get jobs to provide for their family but for insanely cheaper wages

For mediocre crimes, many were tricked, convicted,
imprisoned, and locked in cages

Forced to live in poverty, with only jobs that were of servants and maids
White children being breastfed from a black woman's
breast and also assisting to raise

Despite being treated like dogs, men enlisted and served in
the military, still getting the same unfair treatment
The names *boy, wench, gal, bitch,* and *nigger* was
constantly used to make fun of and offend
Being that slavery was no more, a new group by the name
of the Klu Klux Klan brought in a new fear
With the help of the silent movie *Birth of a Nation,*
another terror season was put into gear

Thousands and thousands found hanging lifelessly from the branches of big trees
Mothers still begging and pleading for their children's life while in their knees

The horrific face of Emmitt Till was publicly displayed
across the country and eventually the world
That was his shameful fate all because of a lie being said
about him allegedly whistling at a white girl

Every black person with a backbone that stood their ground
and fought back was murdered and taken out
Forcing the black people to yet again think of the
consequences and take a different route

It did get to a point where the black people acquired
certain rights and moved a few steps ahead
But that didn't stop the never-ending horror of them turning up dead

With the help of educated brothers and sisters, the Black Panther party was formed
Turning the race relations and revolution into the perfect storm

With the help of informants, traders, and the U.S.
government, that era was sadly short lived

Flooding the black neighborhoods with drugs, causing
self-inflicted damage, forever a negative

With no strong leaders, the drugs and mouse traps set,
Willie Lynch's legacy continued to prosper
Leaving the black people with a life full of struggle,
hurt, death, terror, a straight disaster

The paleface people got smart, only to use tactics to go
from a physical slavery to a mental slavery
Between the U.S. government, the local police, the everyday
citizens, and sadly the blacks, there was absolute no safety

Sad to say that till this very day, the black people are still
seen and treated as second-class citizens
With the aid of the Thirteenth Amendment, they are the ones
who are the vast majority in the countless prisons

A terror act against the tribesmen can be seen or heard about almost every day
Murder, trumped-up charges and sentences, qualified
denied jobs are the ordinary ways
When you thought it couldn't get any worse, any openly sexist and
racist paleface was given the title and power of being the president
This unfortunately opened the flood gates for white supremacists
It began to be open season on the tribesman
Are you getting the gist?

Black tribesman murdered and slain as if it's just the thing to do
Unarmed men, hardworking mothers, innocent child and live on the internet too

The police killing of the black tribesman and getting paid time off
it was different for the black police officer who didn't get off

The prisons they have installed are nothing but modern-day plantations having
eighty percent of their prisoners being black thousands of black lives a-wasting

This place called Amerikkka has been nothing but an open prison and a living hell
The life of a black tribesman is a horror story, nowhere near a love story or fairy tale

The story I'm telling is at its end, but I assure you,
there's so much more I didn't mention
Like the thousands of black women and children who have suddenly gone missing

So don't take this story lightly or think it is made up
because that for sure is not the case
I simply wanted to share with you the story of the nightmare on my race

AN ANGRY BLACK MAN

I am an angry black man, but I don't let it get the best of me
I am an angry black man if only you can see what my eyes have seen

I am an angry black man
To most, all you see is a destructive and bitter man
I am an angry black man
To others, I guarantee my feelings are something you won't ever understand

I am an angry black man simply because of all the pain and
torment that white suppressors have placed on me
I am an angry black man because of your cold heart and also your lack of empathy

Because I am an angry black man, I don't want your sympathy
Empathy goes much deeper
I am an angry black man
I don't want your phoniness, your two- faced or your love either

Because I am an angry black man, I'm aware of how your so-
called love is nothing but poison, a straight-up cancer
Because I am an angry black man, all I want from you is solitude and peace
It's god you have to answer

I am an angry black man because you know that you
pull the strings and cause the earth to rotate
I am an angry black man, but I know the value of human life,
something you can't and won't ever appreciate

I am an angry black man because you always find some
trick or scheme to keep me and my people down
I am an angry black man because throughout history till now,
it's clear to see all the cancer you have spread around

I am an angry black man because you just won't stop
being evil, Satan's helper as I call it
Because I am an angry black man, I curse you to receive
back tenfold all the agony that you set out to inflict
I am an angry black man who prays hard that this madness
and hell finds its way solely back to you
Because I am an angry black man, I shot out to all the bishops
and pastors, even the ones who practice voodoo too

I am an angry black man, but my heart is forever
warm and continues to want peace for all
I am an angry black man, but I won't lose my faith in the Almighty, causing me to fall

It's because of your actions and factions in my life
It's no wonder I ultimately became an angry black man

Because I'm an angry black man, I'm no pushover or fool,
A straight warrior for this you better understand

You can push people so much to the point where they have
nothing to lose and become an angry black man
Your reign is limited and coming to an end
Get ready for a fight, a fight with an angry black man

BETTER MATERIAL

If you've heard my words before, you'd know that I
talk about injustice and racial inequality
But that's a subject that follows me every day and that's glued to me

I would love to talk about other things such as gay happenings and sweet love
But I'm stuck in a world that's full of everyday fight where I have to push and shove

Give me a better life for me and my race, then my words will and can change a bit
From the ancient Jews, Native Americans, Polish Jews, black
Americans till now, we're still getting the same shit

I understand that history repeats itself, but this here is ridiculous
Hasn't anyone learned by now that racial and religious persecution is wrong?
Isn't it obvious?

From reading history books and even the Bible, I can't
understand why mankind would keep that going
Persecuting the next man or woman for whatever reason as if not knowing

Ever really listen to reggae?
Do you hear the pain in their voice and what they're crying about?
Listen to it again
Yes, they are singing, but really they are sad and crying out

Old negro spirituals, hhmm, the truth is in the name itself
Keeping God in their corner at all times when they need help

And now here we are in this year 2016
The fact that these songs, poems, and hymns are still being written is just obscene

Some people have the nerve to say that they're tired of hearing about it
That's really easy to say from someone who doesn't have to live it

That's one of the biggest problems
If it's not done to you, it really isn't your concern
Try crossing over into someone else's life
Feel their pain and strife
Go deep and learn

I'm sharing these words with you because, one, I'm
tired of living it and writing about inequality
Two, I'm sharing these words to those who still
refuse to open their eyes widely and see

See how inequality hurts families and cultures for generations and generations
See how it's so very hard to love someone who hates you, a constant frustration

I've had my share of racial inequality served to me more than I cared to ever have

Even had a heartbreaking situation that sent me on an emotional rollercoaster path

I hope that you are digesting these words that I a m feeding you
I hope that you feel all the pain and frustration that this mess can do

Although hunters and prey, animals in the jungle can live in harmony
Why can't we?

It's not a dog-eat-dog world, more like people-eat-people world
Isn't that crazy?

Living the life I live isn't nowhere near easy
My being here today is both a blessing and a miracle
I simply wish, want, hope, and pray for a better and
prosperous life, a life with some better material

BLACK

Black, what does that mean to most people?
Black, is it something very difficult, or something really simple?

Black is in fact a shade of color or a mixture of them all
Black, according to history and archaeology, it's the race that started it all

Black is in fact a term most Europeans find frightening and also scary
So insulting when you look up the term black in *Webster's Dictionary*

Foul, dirty, evil, wicked, and *demented* are just a few examples
found in the dictionary defining the color black
It's funny yet again insulting that something that people
are afraid of is always the prey of their attack

I challenge you to research the dictionary of the two terms *black* and *white*
It's not hard to figure it out for yourself
It's wide open and in plain sight

What does *black* mean to me when I think about it?
Hmmm, I'm so glad you asked
Black is a wondrous and powerful term, with solidarity
and strength that will forever last

You see, there must be something great about black that Caucasians
will do any and everything to keep the term *black* down
When they're the true cancer spreading evil all over the globe
I mean all around

Melanin is really the true source of being black
It's where the cosmos's energy all stems from
It's better to know the full truth rather than walking around ignorant and dumb

It's very funny how the black race is hated, but so many can't wait
to secretly get an intimate taste of it for their pleasure
Locking our men away and turning them gay, secretly stealing our precious treasure

A fact remains true that without black, there would not be many things on this earth
Responsible for many creations and innovations,
we're talented by nature and by birth
The first man, black, math, black, geometry, black,
systematic ruling, black, Egypt, black, Jesus, black
These are not opinionated words
Everything I speak is one hundred percent fact

We're not just a group of thoroughbreds that can run and can shoot a basketball
Our minds are equipped with a powerful brain, innovating
ideas which Caucasians always take credit for

Black is very beautiful
I dare anyone to say or speak otherwise
Deep down in their hearts, there is love for the black race as well as their spite

Look around you
Our culture is flourishing in the entire world on every level
Hip-hop adored by all, daps and handshakes, urban slang
all being adopted by the common white devil

Wanna have big butts and sun tanning too, trying hard to look like the black race
Cornrows and dreadlocks being filtered in, really, it's a damn disgrace

Can't stand the thought of us but can't help but imitate us
Is it love or is it hate?
Lying to your spouse about staying at work late just
to go on a chocolate and intimate date

So with all this being said, it's clear to see how great black really is
There's a lot of greatness about my race
Take a look at history
There's more positive than negative

The facts speak for themselves
Black is truly beautiful, adored, and loved by all no
matter how you try to downplay black
With our Moorish background and the Most High
on our side, we will always stand tall

COULD YOU STAND IT

My actions and the things I say lead people to thinking I carry myself in a racist way
If they were to take one day out of my life, they'll see what it's like on a day to day

They that everything's cool and that everything's okay either not
knowing or closing their eyes to what is in fact still going on today

Sheets and hoods have been traded in for nightsticks and badges
Police and politicians are all involved, a new American order
That's all that is
Can't go to the store without someone watching or following you
All I wanted was some toothpaste and some milk
What the hell did I do?

For no reason at all, police run your tag and shine the searchlight in your car
Tired as hell, getting off work, haven't broken any laws
This has gone way too far

Been working the same job for years and can never move up the chain
Eventually, they didn't want me anymore, so I got
fired by my boss, the boss that I trained

Even my fiancé, after receiving her degree, the amount of
applications she's filled out, you can't even imagine
Even with her educational background, jobs she was guaranteed
were turned away when they saw the color of her skin

I then look back on all the jobs I've had, and all of the big executives were white
Sure, there were a few black leads and supervisors, but to see
a black person running the operation, not one in sight
There's a new statewide exam that's been implemented
in order to graduate from high school

Ironically, only the black schools are the ones who are
failing, making us look like the dummy and the fool

A labor union back home where six figures can be made
easy also has the weight on their shoulders
What used to be an all-black union has been infiltrated,
run down, and completely taken over

If you listened to everything I said, you would see that life
as a black individual can be truly fucked up
With the only things to keep us going is our aspirations,
determination, God, and simply pure luck

Everything that's been spoken is absolutely true, so don't take any of this for granted
If you think this is all bullshit and it doesn't hold water, come
on into my life, and let's see how long you can stand it

DIVIDED WE STAND, UNITED WE FALL

There once was a time when the word *united* actually stood and meant something
Today, that is something that is no longer, is past tense, and sadly, has been

When there was a cause or problem, we as black people actually stood together
Always having each other's backs no matter the storm nor the weather

I guess you can say it was because we were all equally fucked and trapped
Your story was my story
We both had the same torment and the same wrath

We've been equally screwed, equally lynched, equally raped, and equally slaved
The entire race as a whole is way more important than your own life to selfishly save

The Montgomery Bus Boycott showed the world what
a group can do when on the same page
But all that changed when you approach the weak
and selfish with a compensable wage

And there lies the initial and overall problem
Some people are all about self, dismissing the bigger
cause and problem, no care of the wealth

Of others, they could care less, condemning them to an even deeper pit
With us as a race, it's no wonder why we still get the shameful fate that we get

Brothers and sisters in all black marching and fighting to the same beat,
never giving in or falling to their knees, always standing tall on their feet

That's why Hoover and the government had to shut down
the Black Panther party for self-defense
Entitling us all to have a new strategy in this game, keeping us behind the fence

We really had something good in the sixties and seventies
It was truly one for all
But all it took was that one traitor, that Uncle Tom, to help our entire race fall
Making America great again, we still have them same
Uncle Toms going to the White House
While we are boycotting, a certain company or product,
this buffoon buys the entire store out

We did have one strong brother who took a knee for what he
truly believed in after being blackballed from the NFL
We still had black artist in the Super Bowl who gave in

Black people, this is total bullshit, and you know it
Get off of your ass
This is not the time to fucking sit

I continue to fight not only for myself but for him, her, and even you as well
For peace and freedom, I'm ready to die
I'm prepared to be convicted and locked up in jail

How are we ever gonna move ahead if we don't stick together?
It's all our problem no matter your status, the place, or whatever

No matter how you look at it, what happens to one affects us all
Unfortunately, we may be divided while we stand
We still are united as we fall

EYEPATCH JUSTICE

I lost a family member recently, a person whom I never met
The course of his murder and the outcome, I will neverforget

My heart is very heavy and also very weary
Every time I think about it, I get extremely sad and teary

No matter what you say, an unarmed boy was fatally shot
Nothing was done at all to deserve the fate that he got
To the family of the Martins, I give them my heart, and I pray for healing
I pray for a day where no one is ever again profiled and no more senseless killings

In my eyes, this doesn't have any dealings with the issue of race
The idea of right, wrong, and responsibility of ones actions is the bigger case

So am I to believe that I cannot walk my streets without
the fear of being profiled, shot, and killed?
I firmly stand behind the Second Amendment but the
Stand Your Ground law needs to be appealed

Some have been convicted and sentenced for shooting themselves,
killing of dogs and even giving a fair warning shot
But to kill another human and rate a not-guilty verdict is
cooking America alive and making life boiling hot

Is justice really a blind system that doesn't see our
differences and judges accordingly?
Or is justice blind only to the truth and common sense that are so easy to see?

MY ANCESTORS' KEEPER

For those who know me and say that I'm very militant and very pro-black,
give me a few moments, and I'll tell you why that's where my heart is at

No matter who you are, we're all a product of our environment
The things we witness and have to go through do reflect on how our lives are spent

I also believe that it is the ones before us who also
play a role in who we actually become
There may be an old hero, a teacher, your dad or mom

There are a few in life's past who helped mold the man
that you know today to be quite honest
I love who I've become
I wouldn't have it any other way

You see, my life has purpose, and my purpose has life casted
and molded together like a medieval blade or knife

I naturally get my ways from my dad, a no-nonsense, hurtfully truthful OG
His attitude was stern and solid, will hurt your feelings with the truth and honesty

He'd give you his last, the shirt off his back
He truly had a gigantic heart, but if you ever crossed
the line, you better exit quick and depart

Huey P. Newton did what was really needed at the
time, and to him, I'm forever grateful
A college student turned civil rights activist with words that were very powerful
He showed the entire world about strength in numbers
and knowledge of rights and laws
He showed our black people how to stand up, pick up a gun, and fight for our cause

Tupac Shakur took the United States by storm
They didn't know what hit them through his influential lyrics
He had a sea of black people listening and following him
Words so powerful, you can literally hear and feel the hurt and pain in his lyrics
The everyday life struggles he talked about, there's no way you could ever dismiss

I must point out that both Huey and Tupac were at a young
age during their involvement in the struggle
Doing whatever they could to right the wrong, speaking
on Capitol Hill, even carrying a pistol

Marcus Garvey brought forth his resistance in the struggle on a political level
as much as empowering the Back to Africa movement, a huge endeavor
He gave us the pan-African flag composed of red, black, and green
connecting all black people together on the same page and the same team

Nat Turner is a man whom I will forever have the highest respect and love for
He became the greatest martyr of our cause, the biggest to ever occur
To be pushed to the limit to sacrifice everything he loved
in order to slay dozens of slave masters
Literally forced to go from "thou shall not kill" to
"kill these crackers and oppressors"

Shaka Zulu was the last king of Africa to be conquered and taken over
He did everything he could by being a juggernaut and a ferocious warrior
He embodied the true nature of having that conquering lion spirit
His dominance was felt all around Africa and Europe
Everyone felt it

With all these mighty men I spoke of, how could I
not embrace their spirit for the cause?
The example has been set
I'm definitely doing my part
This horrific struggle affects us all

Listen to my poems and hear what I'm saying
It's my duty to enlighten my people
But I'm more than words

I'm cocked and stocked
I'm ready for a fight uncivil

The laws of America I study them too
I gotta know what I can and cannot do
It definitely and most certainly starts with knowledge to help us get through

Though one day you may have to do the unthinkable, set
aside the Bible, and take down an oppressor or two
For this fight we're in, I'm prepared to die if have to
I'm prepared take a life myself too

That's the difference between me and others
I'm a true warrior who is a natural-born panther
To assist my people and the way we live, I'll gladly go and kill off this white cancer

But strength is in numbers, and sadly we are far away from having that
The way our people are programmed, we're fucked if they launched an attack

Until that day comes, I continue to educate my people and open their eyes widely
Truth of the matter, we're behind enemy lines
At some point, I will exit this country

You should now understand my way of thinking and the cause behind it
Besides, can you even blame me?
The mold has been broken
This is who I truly am
There's no way you can tame me

This is near and dear for me, no fun and games
I have a deep and bottomless love for my black people
Not just for my people that I'm a true keeper of,
For my ancestors, I will always be their keeper

NIGGA SHIT VS. REAL SHIT

I can't be on no stupid nigga shit
The way my mind works keeps me on the real shit

By real shit, I mean by the shit that means something and holds value
By real shit, I'm talking about the elements that elevate me and also you

You must unlock your brain, and for your own sake, get outta that slave mentality
The world that we know is fairy tale and hokum—it is not the reality

Don't keep circling on and on in life's revolving door
Trust me, there is a way out
There's an entire universe of knowledge and information hidden to shut you out

Yeah, I can run the streets and get that fast yet dirty money
I want the money that's residual and legally revolving around me

T.I. is a prime example of how a true hustler is supposed to
elevate himself, going from the neighborhood dope boy to having
a grand hustle TV show, bringing him much wealth

I'm as athletic as they come
Trust, I can straight leave you in the dust, but what happens
when your cartilage says goodbye, leaving you a bust?

That college degree you will gain is only the start of
the plentiful clients and finance to gain
To think only on dribbling the basketball or scoring
a touchdown is stupid and truly insane

Just so you know, I have a strong passion for the species of women, but
my colleague by the name of Trojan always assists me before I go in

Why have an entire tribe of children if you're never
ever there to mold and raise them?
To leave your own child hanging in this hellacious
world is something I strongly condemn
The world is so much bigger than Jacksonville, let alone the state of Florida
As long as I broaden my mind, there's no telling where new ideas can take ya

Too many brothers and sisters are troubled and boxed in with only living for today
I'm all about building a dynasty that will give my grandchildren a prosperous day

I hear you wholeheartedly, brother, and trust me, I do understand
But there comes a time to throw away that nigga shit and become a grown-ass man

Goodie Mob stated to get up get out and get something
How will you make it if you never even try?
There are some rappers who don't talk about bitches and
money, giving you knowledge to help you get by

But just don't get by, I need you to get over, and dammit, I mean fucking take over
Time ain't ever stopping for you
It keeps ticking while your ass keeps getting older

I truly pray that you digested my words
Now is the time to get off of your ass and go get it
My brother, come take a walk with me and trade that nigga shit in for some real shit

PRODUCT OF MY ENVIRONMENT

I'm a product of my environment, and that won't ever change
While I come at you with a smile, simultaneously I still bring the pain

Took shit from no one, get hit with your gun
At the end of the day you'll see I'm the blessed one

Be cautious when around me, I have an inner demon
If you take a piece of my heart, you'll know where I come from

This wasn't my life's wants but more my life's cards
If it wasn't for my momma and God, I'd be behind bars

I'm a strong black man, so I love my black race
I love macaroni and cheese, so I'm killing this rat race

Caucasians say you sympathize, but I strongly beg to differ
As soon as my back is turned, I'm turned back into a nigger

Gotta work extra hard just to live and eat
I get no days off
I'm on guard every day of the week

Your rules and regulations are ruled to regulate me
I'm sick of this permanent injunction set on me

Yes, you're a slick one, but I'm a can of oil
I fight fire with fire, so your plans are spoiled

Everything isn't physical
No man I'm smarter than that I continue to feed by brain ammo, prepared for attack

My mind is valuable and precious, and that you can't ever have
Keep your hands in your pocket, or I'll extend this jab

This is why I'm pro-black, rocking the red, black, and green
Because of your race of actions, I've evolved into the crackernator machine
This wasn't my intention
I was built on love
I'm a man after God's own heart who sits above

Don't take me for granted being that I'm spiritual first
I'm still a human being who takes revenge for thirst

Energy tells no lies
It's nature's fortune teller
You get what you put out is what I'm trying to tell you

You've held my race hostage, with no meeting and without our consent,
so when the tables turn, remember, I'm a product of my environment

STARS AND STRIPES SWITCH

Can't believe my ears, and I can't believe my eyes
although I can say that I'm not even surprised

Through all the lies and the big-ass disguise
An openly racist guy has been elected to America's greatest prize

Am I angry?
No, I've been angry for way too much of my life
I guess now it's time for America to really see my pain and my strife

You look at me in wonder of how I feel the way I feel, not sincerely
knowing that life as a black person is a very bad deal

Did I think we had a chance to elect a woman president?
Why yes
Throughout all we've been through, somehow, we still come out blessed

When I sit back and really think on it, I realized and
said, "Who the hell am I kidding?"
A black man has had the commander in chief position,
but for a woman, that's just unforgiving

I'm no fortune teller, but I can see in America's crystal ball
Get ready for an uprising and a great American fall

You think we had it bad with this or that president,
hmmph, you ain't seen nothing yet
A return of Reaganomics is where the people has placed their bet

Hurt is what I'm feeling inside, and I'm ready for more pain to come

We have just witnessed the new birth of an Aryan- and male-dominated kingdom

Peace is what I constantly pray for, but war is what I am always ready for
Put on your rosary and knee pads
Stock and cock your guns
We have a lot of chaos in store

This is not the world that I've created
This was drawn up long before my existence
Just like the *Hunger Games*, we've just witnessed a new resistance

Now these are not opinions
I only deal with the facts
These past few months, you noticed your associates' and colleagues' acts

The fact is the new president-elect has insulted
almost everyone in the country and globe
The fact is that the new president-elect, all his racial and
sexist ways have constantly been showed

The fact is that the current first lady is a woman of intellect and class
While the new first lady can be seen online showing all of her ass

The fact is that the new president-elect has ruined thousands
of lives with his selfish and racial business agenda
The fact is that now, a former Grand Dragon is now running for a senate seat
Hhhmmm, makes you wonder

Now I'm not opposed to free speech and to voicing how you truly feel
But his whole platform is becoming of a dictator and a Willie Lynch appeal

That's not to say that his opponent was squeaky clean with no skeletons in her
closet, but at least her background, resume, and the office she ran for closely fit

This is the United States of America
It's the standards it was built on and founded
Land of the free, equal rights, and justice for all is all hokum
This country has forever been divided

Remember the three inalienable rights—life, liberty, and the pursuit of happiness
The truth is in the words
Break down your so-called rights
Do they really make sense?

Trust me, I can go on and on and on about the true
spirit of the United States of America
This American nightmare continues to have its stars
and stripes switched out for a swastika

STREET WALKER LOVE

I love women the same, just like the next man
But there's one thing I can't ever understand

To be intimate and sexual with women is the best
But there's a situation with my black people that needs to be put to rest

If I'm gonna be one on one with a woman, it's gonna be a mutual and free interaction
Anytime I'm approached by a woman selling her goods,
I have to give her an encouraging reaction

I see some very beautiful women walking the streets, trying to score a buck
With all these quick tricks and johns, it will turn into bad luck

Some of these women are very tempting and can be hard to turn away
But I can't roll the dice and chance a life-altering situation
No, not today

One other thing is that nowadays, you can't tell who's a man
Or a real woman
You feeling all great and relieved and find out the one you were with is really a man

Although, their appearance shows that they've had a complicated life
I still see a beautiful woman inside that can possibly be someone's mom and wife

I want much better for all these women
Their body is worth more than they give it
I want our community to help them out and refrain, encourage, and lift their spirit

People, let's help change our community, our culture, and our people
Let's help enlighten, encourage, and put our women higher than any steeple

Our women are worth more than a human value of what's between their legs
The true value of any woman is what is in their hearts and also in their heads

Our women are not sluts, skanks, or whores, so let's not treat them as such
Even if they're wearing a prostitute's uniform, treat them with respect and get
in touch with their heart and let it connect closely and profoundly to yours
That woman out on the corner can easily be your mom or sister, yes, yours

I urge you, all of you, to do better by our women and help show them a better way
No matter what happened yesterday, let's help them
have a blessed and prosperous today

Let's all start thinking with our minds and hearts, not just our pelvic region
Let's show our women true love and chover them into a new and fruitful season

THE HUNTED PREY

To all white people, I truly don't expect for you to understand what I'm about TO say
I mean how could you understand my struggles when you've
always been the predator and never the prey?

Sure, you prey on each other at times for whatever may be the reason,
but the game of hunting white people has never been in season

You get upset with me and have a million excuses for
white cops slaying black men and women
Justifying all of thievery actions every time, again, again, and again

What if, just what if the tables were turned, and you had to
be extra cautious just to walk down the street?
What if you had to always be on alert and watch everything you do
just to keep from being killed or, if lucky, severely beaten?
What if you had to seriously talk to your kids, giving them
survival skills in hopes that they make it home?
What if a hoodie, a toy gun, excessive chokehold, or countless
rounds is the reason that your loved one is gone?

Think about how I feel after watching the news to find out that
yet another black slaying has happened in America

I got to be honest
I see red
I want blood, and I want vengeance
I'm past the point of being crazy and hysterical

Now you see right then how you got a twitch in your
eye when I said I want blood and vengeance
Let me just talk about getting even, righting the wrong
There will definitely be a totally different outcome and circumstance

I have to tread softly and be extra careful when I wake up and leave my home
Crooked cops, politicians, and judges, also nigger-
hating supervisors, all I want is peace
Just leave me alone

Don't tell me how to think or feel
You really don't know my struggle

I wish that you would step outside your cozy, safe, and white bubble

This life, this attitude, and these feelings are things that I never asked for or w anted
Just take one day out of my life for yourself, and you
will see what is like to be the hunted . . . prey

THE WHITE CANCER

There's something about the white race that truly bothers me
The evil that they possess is very clear and very easy to see

Now this doesn't say that all white people are evil
But as a whole, the white race is truly some demonic people

Look back through the course of history
Their evil doings has been written over time
Having murder and true hatred leading the way of their biggest crime

No matter where they go, they bring havoc, chaos, and straight mayhem
There's no limit to the hell that they bring
They don't give a damn

It's ironic that the pilgrims that settled America was escaping religious persecution
Completely wiping out the Native Americans, a complete overtake and ruin

How the hell you come to a new land full of people, but you discovered it?
The story of the pilgrims and Pocahontas let me
know at an early age that they ain't shit

A race of people so damn evil, they bring destruction wherever they go,
always leaving a trail of blood behind so that everyone will know

Takeovers and enslavement are their whole way of life
Every race on this earth has had the taste and feel of their sinister knife

The Chinese people felt the power and evil of the white race, too
Thousands forced to work on the railroad with nowhere to go to

The Polynesian islands, all but one was ransacked, torched, and taken as their own
Tonga is the only island not to be taken over to where they can call home

It's a damn shame that majority of all islands is the territory of the white race
I can't think of one country or island where it hasn't taken place

The continent of Africa and its people have been truly fucked completely
No more is it a vast land of resources belonging to the natives or the royalty

Millions and millions of black lives destroyed and their history erased
A complete and an unstoppable force of genocide was and is the case

All the hellacious acts set upon them, a list bigger than an encyclopedia
set is what the black people received from the white race
Simply put, al living hell is what they get

The massacre that was imposed on the Jews was a very sad fate for them
The actions set upon them took too long for them to be condemned

You always hear about the so-called black-on-black crime
But what about the white-on-everyone crime that's
been going on for a very long time?

If you're gay, broke, so-called trailer trash, or not
bougie elite enough, you're easily cast out
Condemning everyone for being a lil' different is what they're all about

I'm serious about this crap
Seriously, look at all these demented horror movies
People are excited to see people being cut up and
cheer to see people hanging from trees

Saw, Sinister, Truth or Dare are just a few of demented
movies that cast their spell on the earth
There's truly a new evil upon this world that has been given birth

Have you seen some of the action and dramatic movies?
How they have so many cruel twist and turns?
Best friends and even family gets fucked over
Hasn't anyone learned?

I'm writing these words because I have set back and
noticed all of white people's cruel acts
Sympathy, empathy, love, and compassion are things that their race truly lacks

Don't get mad at the messenger
I'm simply recording the facts
There's been a mountain of evil that has been placed on our backs

They've condemned every race and, not to mention, even their own
There's no one they won't mess with
No one gets left alone

The truth of the matter is that the white race is truly a
cancer, destroying everyone they encounter
For a race as a whole to have that much hate really makes you wonder

It's gotten to the point where there are even white
people who are ashamed of their own race
White people versus the world since the beginning of time has been the case

Enough of the praying
It never was or never will be the answer
You have to fight fire with fire when dealing with the evil white cancer

WHEN YOU LOOK INTO MY EYES

When you look into my eyes, tell me what do you see when you look into my eyes?
Do you see what's eating me up inside so viciously

When you look into my eyes what is it that you see?
Do you see joy and happiness or pain and misery?

I'm very curious on what goes on in your mind when passing me by
Am I someone you want to leave alone or give me a try?

If you look closely into my eye s, you will see that I'm shattered and broken
You will also feel all the pain from these words that are spoken

The things that these eyes have seen are not normal and very hard to bear
Living in a world where the common man has no love or any care

My eyes reflect all the racial tension and biased inequality I've had to witness
Still having to endure a confederate America that is not past tense

My heart is always warm but has a side that is quite cold,
praying for peace but always ready for war to unfold

Don't judge me by your personal conclusion or my outward appearance
Things can go either to the left or the right
I'm straddling the fence

When you look into my eyes, you will see a person who is sick
and tired of being sick and tired, tired of living a hellacious
black American life that has never been desired

All these aspects are true facts, not opinions, and it shouldn't be a surprise
To put it straightforward, these are all the things you
can see when you look into my eyes

A RELIGIOUS VIEW

I wanna take this time out to clarify and explain myself fully
After these words you hear, you should be able to fully understand m e

There are many things in this world that I don't ever take at face value
Especially if they are aspects of life that's supposed to give you structure and value
I speak of this because of the faith that I personally possess
What I believe and stand for, I can publicly and openly confess

As a child, while watching the series *Roots*, my eyes were
opened to seeing everything for what it really is
Having me look at Christianity lesser and lesser as a
religion and more and more as a business

I know what you're thinking now, and you have every right to feel what you feel
But to give me a new religion, a new savior and, in the
same breath, spite and kill is a horrible deal
How you're gonna give me a totally new belief and
God but curse me in the same name
So a new religion full of liars, rapists, torturers, and
murderers is the faith that I must claim

This is nothing offensive or disrespectful to my elders and parents
I can't lie to myself
I can't lie to you
I simply can't stand it

Before my ancestors were brought to America, their lives were
flowing good and great to their own satisfaction
Who the hell are you to say that their lives were primitive
and animalistic of a different faction?

I see why the main concept of Christianity is to love and
forgive your enemies no matter what they do to you
Seems more like a strategized plan to love and forget about all the evil done to you

I'm serious,—I always wondered why there have always been missionaries
throughout history spreading the good news of Christianity
With the same thought on why the previous Roman and
Greek religions are more considered mythologies
Out with the old and in with the new, yeah, the New World Order

The new religion, brought upon the entire world just to control order

This goes way beyond Christianity
Its origins goes back to the Egyptians with the worship of Osiris and Amun-Ra
The great meeting orchestrated by Constantine and the
Pope is the real reason why this has gone this far

Again, I see things for their true essence, their true origins
and what is painted elaborately in front of my eyes
How could I not feel some type of way about an underlying evil and conspiracy?
How could I not despise?

Seriously, a person continuously abuses you but
justifies their actions with the same ideology
For you to accept that and never question it, there's
stupid written on your forehead permanently

Again, this is not a Christian bashing or a religious dogging,
just me using my God-given common sense

The days of me accepting given bullshit that you would
give a child is ancient history and past tense

There are many many things that I am, but a fool I won't ever be

Just as easy as it is to smell bullshit, it is also very easy to see

CROWN OF LOCKS

It's funny when I reconnect with old friends I haven't seen in a long time
Like clockwork, there's one thing they can't shake that's on their mind

There's one physical attribute about me that they are quite aware
One of the first things out their mouth is, "Hey, you got hair"

From my earlier days in life, I was known to rock a bald head
The response from the females at the time was all that needed to be said

I had a bald head to look smooth, debonair, and serve a dating purpose
I also rocked a bald head because of me being in the service

But that chapter is old
I'm in a new frame of mind
Along with elevating wisdom, I'm letting my hair grow with time

Some may have dreads for the today's thug or as a fashion sense
I'm growing my locks to show the world I have more than just common sense

I was always taught that to have locks means to have wisdom
To look around at our young children today, they are labeled as ignorant and dumb

I've always wanted to have my hair locked, but I
didn't want the stigma that came with it
After getting a knowledge of self and a deeper
understanding, I had to go through with it

For those who follow my work, you know that I
promote endless research of knowledge
This world is full of information, no need for a college education

If your mind-set is the same from when you were
younger, then you've clearly wasted time
Be better than you were before
Evolve as a person
Upgrade your mind

So that's why I wear my crown of locks with confidence
They protrude from what I have inside   .
To have long locks is a statement, a symbol, and a
culture that should be worn with pride

Having locks is not dreadful
Don't let the European English fool and keep you boxed
I'm not sure about you, but I'm proud to display my beautiful crown of locks

EVOLUTION OF ME

Am evolving as a living being, I am currently shedding my old skin
There comes a time in your life when old ways must end

I am climbing step by step up the ladder of spiritual consciousness
The more I study and read, the more I am overwhelmed with bliss

It has been an amazing and exciting journey I've taken thus far
To find out that we as humans are much bigger than what we think we are

Everything in this world is very well connected, and this I know to be true
So many hidden secrets and mysteries to which there lies the proof

So I must depart from my Pisces ways and embrace the age of Aquarius
This is the rebirth of myself
I'm sprouting out from my own dust

There is no looking back
I've wandered too far down this rabbit hole
I wanna know more and as much as I can
Much more I wanna unfold

Only a few out there who can understand these
words, but many can't even comprehend
No matter what you've been taught, to ask questions is not a sin

This is my farewell to my past
It was fun while it last
Give me a hug while I say goodbye
My chakras are aligned, connected to the low and
high while seeing all through my third eye

FUCKED

We as a people are very much fucked
Fucked with no Vaseline, with not a prayer or any luck

Fucked in a way that you can't imagine the seriousness of it
Fucked in a way that we're literally drowning in shit

What do I mean by us being fucked?
Well, I will explain
Listen to my words carefully, and let them soak into your brain

The world as we know it is nowhere near as what it seems to be
An elite global force spreading nothing but chaos and catastrophe
Controlling every aspect and every way of our life stuck
deep inside of us, deeper than any blade or knife

Everything we know of and think is all hokum and a big-ass lie
It's past time you started asking the questions what, when, where, how, and why

Why does history continue to repeat itself, same mistake after mistake?
How much longer will the human race continue to bend over and take taking
all bullshit, lies, and mixed messages coming from the government
Allowing them to do all sorts of things to us daily with and without our consent

Our elected officials and politicians are selected and present for a reason
This is an ongoing situation, people
Trust me—it's gonna continue to last more than a season

The government has its own agenda, and we the
people are merely pawns and sheep
Placing laws and ideas in our lives continuously to keep you down and weak

The word *democracy* is not exactly what you think it is

It is way more complex
We've all been hoodwinked, bamboozled, led astray, and placed a hex

The laws that we know are not there to protect and defend us
The Constitution is not for your benefit
It never was

We are merely slaves to the government and really on a bigger scale
Your brain and mind are the major products that have always been for sale

These wars and so-called acts of terrorism are nothing but strategized chess moves
Merely ways of control over other elite forces and to gain your trust too

The news and media are all playing their role in this game too
Just another tactic to keep you in line and in control too

You see, if you control the people's mind, anything can be done, people
We have to stand and stick together for once
It can be done but not by only one

Think of this: the wealthiest country in the world is
also the sickest country in the world
What else can I tell you for the truth to finally come out and unfurl?

Ever wonder why there are so much cancer, obesity,
heart trauma, and so much death?
No matter what you do and eat, you will never be in complete and solid health
Everything we consume and eat plays a major part in our well-being
The food industry, FDA, and healthcare system have truly been misleading

Countless GMO products are being served to us on the daily basis
These GMO products lack everything we need, leaving our bodies weak and frail
The products that we do need are not authorized
and exempt from human consumption
Also placing harmful products in everything we use,
making it hard for our bodies to function
The real drugs that are prescribed are there to make you even sicker
They are not produced to make you better, only there to inflict

I urge you to really research the products that you put on and into your body
The real truth behind it all is dangerous, hellacious, and outright scary

The body products, the clothes, the electrical devices all play a major role
There's a big reason why this and that person has cancer, a tumor, and a mole

Look at other third-world countries who are much poorer than we will ever be
The fact that their lives are much healthier and longer than ours
How can that be?

When exposed to thousands of man-made chemicals and products
on the daily basis, it's very hard to escape the deadly end
Again, we're in a chess game that has been strategically designed for us not to win

Even your religious and spiritual views have been
created to harm as opposed to do any good
The whole idea of religion is not what it seems and everyone totally misunderstood

I know I'm cutting deep now on what I am saying
Trust I'm speaking to you facts
I am not playing

Don't get me wrong—I believe and seek guidance from a higher power
Just that a man-made group or religion won't ever
be something I dwell on and devour

Read a book or three and find out how the Egyptians
lived and also who they worshiped
You will quickly find out the origins of our current
religion s and how they came equipped

I urge you to look up and research fully the word *astro-theology*
Trust you will find quite the surprise
There's so much hidden in plain sight, right in your
face, the best way to conceal and disguise

One other thing to consider is that why old Roman and
Greek spiritual ways are taught to us as mythology

You have to use your brain
Use it to its fullest capacity
Thin k for yourself and also think logically

Even God himself said to ask and it will be given
He also said to know and have a complete understanding
The same time you spend on other things in life,
spend just a small time reading a book
It's really not that demanding

Everything I've shared with you came from countless
books, including the Bible and also the Internet
Yes, the Internet has so much information and knowledge on it
Instead of porn, games, and Twitter, try to learn from it

We are in the age of information
Why not take advantage and gather all that you can?
It will benefit you and me

Don't be so closed-minded, ignorant to the real truth
It's time to fully wake up and truly see

See that as a whole, we are in a situation that has us all
delusional and dying slowly while on our knees
As I stated earlier in the beginning, we are being fucked
royally, with no Vaseline, cream, or grease

IGNORANCE

Merriam-Webster's Dictionary defines *ignorance* as
"lacking of knowledge and information"
In the world we live in today, it truly is the product of our miseducation

Yes, we have schools and prestigious universities
where we obtain our knowledge from
The fact still remains that as a whole race of people,
we are blind sheep who are dumb

Majority of information we obtain is gathered from schools and the books we read
But our brains can obtain much more than the
information that our school system feeds

Notice that I used the term *school system*, and there is a reason for that
A system designed to trick you in a way to oppose
the truth, there's so much that we lack

Do you really think that the powers that run this world
are gonna give out all of the information?
In this world we live in, ignorant minds has always
been the the focal point of the occasion

Speaking of information, it is known that we do live in the age of information
To that degree, it's time that reading and researching
becomes the priority of our generation

Knowledge has been and always will be the source of
all power to get a clear understanding of life
It is the thing that our brains must devour

I challenge all creeds of people to read a book or two instead of wasting time
To deny people's right to knowledge and information, to me, is the biggest crime

You're upset and frustrated with the government and the things that politicians do
At the end of the day, the only person responsible for your frustration is you
Because you never took the time to understand how
government really works and how its run
You will forever be upset about the things that occur
while you sing the same sad song

Believe me when I tell you, majority of everything we've
been taught is all a big and tremendous lie
With the sheep of people walking around blindly never asking the question why

You see, it's so easy to control people when you control the information that is given
Forever keeping people and their minds in a delusional state and fairy-tale prison

A prison is where you will always be in if you continue to
be ignorant and never search for the hidden truth
Knowledge will set you free permanently simply because you
have undeniable evidence that shows your proof

It brings me much joy to enlighten and inform people of
the information that was never given to them
It brings me an even bigger joy to debate someone who thinks they know
it all and, with the knowledge I share, turn their light from bright to dim
At the end of the day, ignorance is very damaging
It will ruin your entire life and the way you think
Keeping you deep down below the surface of the
ocean where you will continue to sink

Don't stay forever in the box created for you
You'll miss out on where your life went
To stay ahead of the game being played, keep your mind
informed and please refrain from being ignorant

INCARCERATION

Incarceration, what is it for real?

One thing's for sure, it's definitely the real deal
I want to share with you a few words on how detrimental incarceration can be
Open your ears and open your mind
Take in what I'm saying and truly see

People being locked up every day for this and that crime,
getting countless years, taking away their time
Time is essential to everyone on this earth
Taking away from people the part that's really worth

My time is very precious, so I cannot ever just throw it away being
a slave for the government and state, not now, no way
Yes, you heard me correctly
I did say *slave*
Oh really, you didn't know?

This is nowhere near my opinion, the Thirteenth Amendment told me so
Take the time to read your Constitution
It's right there in black and white
Read it slowly and thoroughly and get the correct insight

Although incarceration is a physical aspect of slavery, there is really so much more
There is a constant mental slavery that's absolutely nothing to adore

Yes, I do have my freedom, and I can say this and mean it true
To keep my body and mind free, there's nothing I wouldn't do

Do read, research, and investigate every aspect of this life
It will alleviate, rid, and cease any stress, any hard time, any strife

48

You see, I refuse to be a slave to anyone or any state or government
I'm a man of self-worth, self-preservation, and with both, I'm very content

Though being physically locked up is enough to drive any person crazy and insane
The greatest part of anyone that can be ever taken away is their brain
You take away a person's mind and then you have taken away everything

For those who are able to have their third eye open is truly a blessing
The mind is the most precious thing we own, and it shouldn't ever be taken away
It belongs to you and only you
Hold on to it
What more can I say?

If you ever saw the movie *The Matrix*, there is a powerful message in that movie
Open your mind to see the real truth
Don't need your eyes
Your brain allows you to fully see

We all are incarcerated in some sort of way
It's up to you to find out what cards to play

Incarceration is truly a crutch and can be damaging and damning to you
Just give every action of your life a second and third thought before anything you do

There are many people and many powers that can't wait to own and incarcerate you
Keep your freedom
Keep your mind
Incarceration is hard to get out of but easy to get into

IT'S WHAT YOU KNOW

I'm a research enthusiast and an information junkie
I stand by and live by it
How am I ever supposed to grow if I never feed my brain?
I can't grow off of eating shit

There's so much information that are hidden in words and hiding in plain sight
Just pick one subject and research it thoroughly
I promise you'll have a new insight

Since people don't read, it's the easiest way to game, ensuring that you never win
It's no wonder we're in the shape that we are in
It's a cycle that never ends

You gotta step outta the box and inspect it thoroughly
There are some hidden jewels
Use your main tool to discover what's been hidden
I'm telling you there are many more tools

We're all trapped in a world that's full of deception
It's the fuel that keeps it going
Using ignorance as leverage and stupidity as gas, keeping you from not knowing

Read everything you can and also study the dictionary
Stop being played for a dummy and fool
You're small but a valuable pawn in this game to ensure a profitable rule

From experience, I can tell you that having knowledge
is definitely power and the key
The look on their face when you throw facts back, a priceless thing to see

You gotta let them know that you're on your shit,
and you're there to go blow for blow
It's said that it's who you know
In all actuality, it's really what you know

PUBLIC SERVICE ANNOUNCEMENT

I wanna clarify my thoughts and the way I think
Pay attention to everything I say and don't even blink

If you know me, you would know that I can be considered somewhat controversial
The truth is that I only give and speak true facts, facts
that won't be found in school or an infomercial

You see, I pride myself on always reading, researching, and searching
Searching for the buried truth, the truth that's so out of
this world, it may leave your head hurting

It's so amazing what you will find out when you simply open up a book
Causing you to stop and give this entire world a
whole second and, at times, a third look

I'm saying these words so the blind and lost will stop
looking at me like I'm the crazy one

Wow, the one who reads is the crazy one for using his brain as
opposed to the billions who are ignorant and dumb

Look around you and take a deeper look inside
The truth is always revealed
It can't ever hide

Do you really think that the powers that be are honest and straight up with you?
This whole world is a fairy tale and hokum
It's all planned out, even your life too

Think I'm joking, research about social security numbers and what they're really for?
Behind everything we encounter, there's a monetary and
bloody reason stored behind a closed door

The medical industry and the FDA play a very big part in this matrix of life
Ensuring you stay sick, unhealthy, and broke, at times
possibly giving an abrupt stop to your life

These so-called wars we engage in are nothing but
foul play and a strategized chess moves
An agenda so evil and corrupt that it's is damn near
impossible to correct and improve

The president of the United States has never ever
been decided by the common people
Your voice and vote truly doesn't exist
I really hope this is sinking into your head and your temple

Pay close attention to all of the movies you watch and even the music videos
The fact that they are portrayed from the reality of this
world where only a certain few only knows

All the stars, politicians, and corporate big wigs are all in cohesion
Same hand signs, same ideas, same evil agendas
are all done for the same exact reason

To be honest, running this hellacious world is merely
six families with the world in their hands
Certain bloodlines controlling every factor of our lives
has always been the New World Order's plans

What I'm gonna tell you next may cause you to stop
reading and totally have ill thoughts about me
These are true facts
Don't kill the messenger
Again, go pick up a book, research and see

Your beloved religious views, Holy Bible, Holy Koran, and
your precious born-again Savior are all lies
A man born of a virgin caused many miracles, walked on water,
died for our sins, and no one questioned how or why

Research and study world religions, the history and the origins of them all
Placing a controlling philosophy over the mass of people
with religion was and is still our biggest downfall

Don't get me wrong
I am truly a man of God, and he is the only one whom
I pray to and have a spiritual connection to
But to pray to a false demigod or ask for forgiveness from the
pope and kiss his hand is something I just won't do

The truth and signs are all there, hidden in plain sight, read
your Bible carefully, so many lies that give the truth
If you know anything about Osiris and Egyptian history, it's the same exact story
There is your proof

Look at the Kennedys, Martin Luther King Jr., Malcolm X, and Bob Dylan
Ever wonder why they were killed?
That was the result of them relaying the truth to the public
The powers that be had to collect on that bill

On that note, if I mysteriously die tomorrow, it would be because
I shared these words to the people without their consent
I'm not afraid of death
We all have to go
These words are too crucial to get out on this public service announcement

REAL PEOPLE

It's funny how people look at me crazy on some comments and the things I have
to say but keep a tight lip when politicians and white people send bullshit our way

Quick to take offense and have a rebuttal for when the small black man speaks

But the controversial statements are made by the president damn near every week

Nothing is what they do, giving a blind eye to the situations that really matter

Ignorantly not seeing or accepting why this country and
government are fucked up and in a disaster

Why single me out and have a comment to say to me?
Why not comment on the bullshit that even Stevie Wonder can see

Why get mad with me for speaking up and exercising my First Amendment right?
Why are you not calling the leaders on their bullshit that's in plain sight

You wonder why things are in shambles and the country is the way it is
It's people like the mutes and do-boys that keep the growing cancer of negative

People, you have a voice
You have a brain
Use them daily as opposed to being the American slave that you are

It's your life—fight for it
That's reason enough
No wonder why it's lasted this long, this far

Now if you are all about self, certain groups and clicks, then
kill yourself and make the world a better place

Political parties, race, ethnic backgrounds, gender
have been for too long the American case

So here it is, the man who gives a damn about himself is
ignorant and don't know what he's talking about
Giving me hell and bullshit just because I have a
backbone and not afraid to voice and shout

So look at the facts that's in front of you and take them for what they are really for
The fact remains that there are people like me who are real
This country could use many, many more

Real people

SICK AND TIRED

I'm so sick and tired of this constant bickering and bullshit
Enausiated of the ever going separation of a species, it makes me so sick

It's 2013, and the world is eating itself up
Those who are in power are more than ever fucked up

Black, white, yellow, brown, straight, gay, Democrat, Republican, old, and young,
everyone being singled out for their difference instead of being united as one

I can't take this shit no more
It's really getting under my skin
Being discriminated against on all levels over and over again

Can't go to our leaders
Hell, they're the main fucking problem
Though it's gonna take more than laws to come through and solve them

The phrase "In God We Trust" is misused
Such crap and a total lie
Just take a closer look in the Constitution's Bill of Rights
And you'll see why
"Life, liberty, and the pursuit of happiness" is what it states right there in your face
The way we've all been divided and led astray is really a big disgrace

I do pray for peace and a world where everyone will always be accepted as one
I pray for a day when all the racist, sexist, religious
and political bullshit is over and done

THE AMERICAN PIMP

I am a whore, but not the kind that you're thinking
I'm the whore that's been pimped since birth, forever keeping me sinking

Yes, ever since I got a social security number, I've been getting pimped
Trying to get over and overcome has yet to prevail and hard to attempt

You see, I'm a whore of the establishment with my pimp being the U.S. government
Yes, you heard me right, pimping me faithfully with
no remorse, sorries, or repentance

Of everything I earn, I have to give them a piece of it
I worked hard for that eight dollars
This is bullshit

I understand the fair-share tax to keep our country afloat
But all this extra, excess, and nonsense taxes, I'm not with
They got to go

Can't do this and can't do that, can't get assistance because of red tape
I tell you, my ass is raw and damn near bleeding from all of this rape

Now it's not just the government that's raping and pimping me out
Keeping up with the light bill, electricity, and water, uuuggghh, I have to shout

I can't even afford to get sick, let alone have decent insurance
Charging me $30 for one damn aspirin, and not even with my consent

It's truly a crime on how the insurance and medical industry fucks us all
Designed for us to never really get better, just patchwork while they watch us fall

Even American veterans who risked their lives, some torn
limb to limb, literally get fucked every way possible

A lot living on the street, dishonored and dismissed

Disloyalty

The oil industry is very much getting its entire piece of the American pie
with everyone at the gas pumps screaming out why in the hell can't we
adopt similar practices of other countries that use a train system
I've seen it for myself
Nobody's paying high gas prices
A monthly $70 is their premium

To eat here is damn near a sin of the things we put into our body on the daily basis
The average meal is full of crap and cheap, but having
to pay way more just to eat healthy

Even to get higher education for a job that's not promised is damn near not worth it
Even the president just recently paid off his college loans, forty years later
That's bullshit

I can honestly go on and on about all the big pimps
that we have here in America, but I digress
To live in this place we call home, it's really a shame,
a shamble, and a complete mess

I'm man enough to say these words simply because
it's the truth and I'm far from a wimp
I'm just tired of being on the stroll and fucked by the American pimp

TO SEE OR NOT TO SEE

There's a song that came out a while ago called "Vice Versa"
It focused on the concept of opposites, like things that love ya and curse ya

There are many things that we know simply because we were taught
There are other things that we will never know, and they can't be bought

It's funny yet sad to see the human race fighting and killing over a person's religion
Fighting over something that has control over everyone
on the earth, I mean total dominion

I'm sick of being ridiculed and fussed at just because I see with all three eyes
People so hung up on what they believe in that they
look at me like I have an evil demise

I hear it all the time, that I need to keep the devil
out and go back to what I was taught
I'm no devil worshiper
I'm just continuing my journey of knowledge, getting from under this rock

By *rock*, I mean stepping out and looking outside
of the box that we as a whole are in
Believe me—if you really read and research, you will sadly
find out how we've been lied to time and time again

I do pray for my family and loved ones who live their lives in the dark
The Most High up above is who I believe in
There's no satanic nature in my heart

A higher deity I do believe in and pray to
There's nothing that will turn me aw ay
I simply stand for learning the plain truth and the true origin
That's the direction I sway to

For instance, just think, that if what was good was really
bad and what was bad was really good
What if everything we were taught and learned was taken
out of context and totally misunderstood?

I'm saying all this because of what I've found out from my extensive reading
It's been a hard pill to swallow, but so much I've been
taught has been nothing but misleading

I *over*stand that the majority of our people has been programmed and
brainwashed to believe the everyday customs and traditions
But there comes a time when you have to open your third eye and think
for yourself, throw that rod back in the lake and keep fishing

This is nothing negative to my elders and preachers who raised me from a child
I always took them seriously and learned but constantly
questioning everything all the while

Wisdom is not just from age and experience
You can gain it from reading and constantly feeding your brain
To accept everything at face value and never question anything, to me, is just insane

So don't formulate your conclusion about me, especially when
there is so much that you are ignorant and blind to see

There are some of us who continually educate ourselves as opposed
to those who keep their eyes closed, choosing not to see

TRUE LIES

Ignorant, in the dark, lost, hoodwinked, led astray
All of these describe the American minds of today

We think we're so superior above others and have all the power and knowledge
The fact remains that there are many things that will
never be taught in school or college

Though you possess prestigious degrees, countless
books, and you feel towering over all
Compared to the true knowledge of history and
current affairs, you know nothing at all

This is not against the American people in any kind of way
It is against the education and political leaders who
Lie on almost everything they say

It's really simple if you stop and really look at all things at face value
The fact of the matter is that majority of the concepts
given are there only to mislead you
Ever look up the word *conspiracy*?
Research it and see its true definition
You will quickly find out why we as a whole are in our current position

I would never say overthrow the government or become a vigilant or radical
Just pick up a book or two and research for yourself
Feed your brain
That's all

Don't be ignorant to the big truth that has us all blinded and dumb
There's so much more going on in life than wasting it a way on nonsense and fun

Don't get me wrong—I like to have fun and enjoy life myself

But my main concerns in life are learning the truth and also preserving my health

There is so much going on that the public wouldn't have a clue on
Conspiracies and mass propaganda on all levels been
going on before you were eve n born
Again, I urge you to pay close attention to all that goes around you
Pay attention to the current events and all things that occur in the news

The news that is given is deeper then you can ever, ever imagine
The fact of the matter is that there are many lies fed
to you constantly time and time again

A wise man once said that if there's anything important, place it in a book
All the information is evident
It's up to you to research and look

All I want is for everyone to open their minds and be
open to the reality that's in front of their eyes
Believe me when I tell you almost everything we know
and have been taught is truly habitual lies

A DIFFERENT ROUTE

I'm at a crossroads, but these crossroads I've been here before
This time I must take a new direction, making my own detour

I've been down this road for far too long
I have to change direction before everything I love is gone

It's taken me some years to get to this point in my life
I'm tired of the same speed bumps, fender benders leaving me in strife

I've had some close calls and some serious accidents too
I'm ready for a better route in life, something beautiful, something new

I can't ever look back into my rearview mirror
There's too much pain
The lessons will always be remembered to help me
I have so much to gain

It's very sad that it's taken me this long to get on the right route
No more drunk driving, cruise control, or willy-nilly driving about

My vehicle is all tuned up and also has a full tank of gas
If any hot rod, BMW, or stretch limo comes up, I'll just let them pass

I've finally got my act together, and I would like to keep my license
I'm keeping the speed limit, no rush
I will keep her in my presence

This life we live has many different roads and routes
We must drive carefully
Trust me, most roads I've taken were back roads that were exciting but deadly

I will no longer risk the lives of mine and others on the road
There's a whole different route waiting just for me to open and unfold

CHANGE YOUR COURSE

So you say you didn't get hired simply because of your race
But you walking around with all those tattoos on your face

You say no one wants to be around or even hang out with you
But your insides are foul becoming of your disgusting attitude

You complain that you got looked over for the new position
But you being prompt and on time for work has been nonexistent

You're upset that your father is beating and mistreating your mother
But your lyrics are filled with derogatory thoughts of women like no other

You say you're tired of the politicians and the way the government is being run
But the number of times your name is on a casting ballot, not even one

You say you want a better life for you and for your family
But your daily routine is drinking, smoking, and PlayStation 3

You say you wanna lose weight and get back to your high school size
But your daily diet consists solely on doughnuts,
quarter-pounders, and cheese fries

You say you're tired of dealing with your baby momma's stress and nagging
But you wanted to be a big player, getting all the women and not even strapping up

Mike already told us in the eighties for us to start with the man in the mirror
Do all that you can to turn your life around and make the right detour

I'm not here to pass judgment or point fingers
That's not my job or purpose
I'm just stating the facts, the facts that may help you change your life's course

CHOICES AND DECISIONS

Choices and decisions, two things in life that we face on the daily basis, not
knowing which is right, but our choices seem to always end up in a failure

You try to do the right thing, and at times, that doesn't go the correct way
Sometimes your choice may give off the impression that all you want is to play

Yes, we've all made some bad decisions that we can never be proud of
Causing you to look like a black and hungry vulture instead of that white dove

There are many choices in my life that I wish I could take all back
There are some decisions I made that make me feel like sweaty shit in a sack

Sometimes my decisions really hurt and upset the ones I love and care for
With wishes and prayers to god above to try my best to never hurt them any more
At times I sit back and look at all the bad choices I've made
For some of those choices, the high prices of them are constantly being paid

I do ask God for forgiveness and also from the ones it affected
I ask God for a new way of life, a new heart, a new man resurrected

From the deepest part of my heart, God knows that I
am sincerely sorry for my wrongdoings
I hope and pray that our great and wonderful friendship doesn't end up in ruins

THE DEATH OF MYSELF

There's a lot that we go through in life that keep us drained
At times, they leave us confused, lost, and at times hard to keep life maintained

The dilemma I've been dealing with is not a new one for any man
Sit back for a minute, and I'll help you understand

Let me speak for myself
I am a good person with a warm heart
But I've had a life where I've picked up women like shopping at the local mart

It is what it is, and I'm not giving any excuses
Leaving me with with a bad hand like a pair of deuces

No matter what I do or where I go, there's some new woman that comes into
my life, constantly going down the same road even though I had a wife

That's where my dilemma gets rough and very hectic
Not even thinking with my head
Instead, again thinking with my dick

This is a life that I have tried to reverse and change
Though impossible to see, becoming a better man has been my aim

You can say that I'm weak in the flesh or simply weak minded
In the end, my actions got my marriage expelled and suspended

Seems like every time I go for the straight and narrow, again enters another woman
If this was a crime, I'd definitely be doing eight to ten

This is a lifestyle I don't want and certainly not proud of, always
praying for help and forgiveness from the Lord above

I've even had instances where I've done some things
that I wouldn't let hit the light of day on
Locked in the closet and dungeon forever is where those skeletons will stay

My dilemma has had me stressed out for too many years and too many days
Deep in my heart, I really want to change my hoeish and selfish ways

Some may say, "just do better
It's not hard and look at me in shun"
I hear you loud and clear, but hear me when I say it's easier said than done

I've hurt so many people whom I've come across,
and someday I hope that I'm forgiven
I pray for solidarity and peace, praying I don't get cut short living

In the end, it is a bed that I have made, and only I can lie in it
I'm not giving up my fight
I'm moving forward
I'm in it to win it

This has been a very hard road, and I have the accident reports to prove it
I'm not ashamed to say it, but I need assistance and God as my copilot

I can say that God has intervened, come in my life, and showed favor
But the pain I caused still lingers around just for me to hold and savor

This is my plea, my proclamation, my cry for help
Will women be the death of me, or will I be the death of myself?

GOD, IF YOU GET ME OUT OF THIS

How many times were you in a situation when you said,
"God, if you get me out of this . . ."
For those of you who can't count them, including
myself, remember ignorance is bliss

Grown men and women going through life as if they are fifteen and sixteen
Constantly and habitually doing the same thing
but crying for help the times between
Coming across horrific and sometimes deadly crossroads on the day to day
I'm not perfect myself
I'm still fighting my own personal crossroads
This I can openly say

But what if we all kept going straight as opposed to turning to the left and right?
What if we kept on his path, the path of eternal light?
What if we continued to hold on and use everything that we were taught?
What if we used what god already placed inside us, inside our souls and our hearts?

For those who are parents, you know how it feels for a
defiant child begging you to bail them out
I'm so thankful I serve a God who is always there, never to shut me out

It's time to stop taking God for granted
Do what's right and stop always asking for help
Those who know me know that I am no preacher, but I am preaching to myself

If we ever stop getting into that, we wouldn't have to ask God to get us out of this
If we stay on his path of righteousness, God has so
much in store than we could ever ask or wish

HURTING MY FATE

This is about being hurt and hurting someone else
This hurt is not good at all and always casts evil spells

No one wants to get hurt, but we all go through it
The worst is when you hurt the one you love, which stings more than a bit

Why do we hurt each other?
I cannot answer this question
I'm still learning that many things in life need to be put into discussion

I have hurt people in my life, and I'm nowhere near proud of it
I'm here to change my evil way in front of everyone, and I will stand by it

I had someone incredibly special to me, and I truly fucked it up
I'm tired of this racket
I can't lose anyone that important anymore
I have had enough

I can't believe my actions
I'm really hating myself now
My heart has been self-inflicted as if I've been run over by a plow

Because of what I did, I don't deserve her at all
I'm just hoping for that chance to fall

Back in love with each other is where I know our destiny will end up
I pray
I pray for that one second chance to show that I've found that better way

Nothing hurts worse than to be the cause of losing the one you're in love with
I'm willing to go broke, give up everything, and always give her the best gift

Love is truly the key to all things in this world
To keep her in my life and keep her happy, I'm ready and willing to give it a whirl

I won't ever, ever, ever again jeopardize a blessing that's been placed before me
I can't afford to lose anyone like her again when everything
is just like her, so beautiful and pretty

This is a hard lesson learned
I just hope that with her, it's not too late
Deep in my heart, I know with no doubts that it's her who is my fate

I'M THANKFUL

With this year coming to an end, I look so much to the new year
There's so much coming my way for the better
Really nothing to fear

The year 2018 was a serious rollercoaster, but I managed to see it through,
Setting me straight and on the right path, knowing exactly what I have to do

As I come into this new year, I'm very grateful and appreciative of what I do have
I'm even more thankful that I didn't stray too far off from the right path

First and foremost, I'm thankful for life
So many didn't make it to this day and time
It feels so good to be able to compare myself to an old bottle of wine

My health is not one hundred percent, but I have it better than him or her
With some of my past actions, I am truly blessed
This I am sure

I'm thankful for having a sane mind and able to get along on my own
I don't even have foreign thoughts in my head
I am solo and alone

I can't appreciate my momma enough
Lord knows she is my steady rock, always in my corner, at times
fighting me to correct me, putting bad spirits to a stop

I'm thankful for my family, even the ones who constantly give me a butt to kiss
They've prepared me to consume anything no matter how cold the dish

I can't be more thankful for my very best friend who
has always played a major role in my world

What we have together is above and beyond special,
enjoying the blossoming of a new world

I'm extremely grateful to have a father figure, badly
needed to assist manning me up when I need it
Although I haven't been the best son, he is a big part
of me now, and I greatly appreciate it
I've truly been blessed to have a globetrotting career
that satisfies my bills and pockets
I'm a long way from slaving for peanuts while half-crazy in my mind and wits

I'm thankful for the few tools and toys that I can say that's all mine, appreciative
for the things I need as opposed to being materialistically blind

It feels good to be able to need so little, to feel so full and complete
I seriously do not need thirty pair of shoes to rotate daily on my feet

I'm truly grateful for the gift of words and expression
that help me cope with pain and hardship
There's nothing sweeter than my passion of musical therapy
I'm soothing myself
Please, no tip

Year 2019 is the grand entrance of the life that I've
dreamed and prayed about so much
I'm definitely gonna be living my best life
I want the same for you as well
Be blessed and good luck

The Most High God has continuously smiled on my life, and
I won't ever stop giving him thanks and praise
I'm thankful for all that I have and don't have
I'm thankful for life and also better days

IN LOVE WITH WOMEN

No one's perfect in this world, and I'm speaking for myself

Some actions have consequences that can damage your finances, family, and health
I have my own personal problem, and I'm man enough to admit it
I pray to God all the time to help me turn around and quit it

This problem that I have is truly that of the flesh of women
No matter what I do to turn away, I find myself back at square one again

Now I'm no Wilt Chamberlain
I could never get that bad, but there are countless women
who've said I'm the best they ever had

No matter where I go or do, I constantly find myself in-between
I guess you can say that my lower head takes over and takes advantage of me

The ones who looked down the road and brought up
marriage, a couple of women come to mind
Also having women scattered across the city and world all at the same time

Probably by now, I Feel that I've gotten your full attention

I even have some grave-takers that I rather not mention

Contrary to popular belief, this is a very heavy burden to carry
What makes it worse is when you have a conscience and also when you are married

I never planned on being that guy or, plainly put, unfaithful

I never planned on taking my wife for granted or showing that I'm not grateful
Don't get me wrong—I'm a very nice guy
Lust is the one thing that I've ever been guilty of

Despite everything I said, I do love my wife, but it's
the flesh of women that I am in love

KNOWLEDGE

I am what separates ignorance from understanding
I am the main aspect in proper planning

I am what little people desire the most
I am what most people hardly know

I am what you need to get ahead in life
I am what gives people more than might

I am what is more valuable than financial gain
I am what will keep a person from going insane

I am what keeps the intellectual person ahead of others
I am what you have been lectured about by your father and mother

I am what will make your life calmer, easier, and stress free too
I am what you'll need to use, but it simply starts and ends with you

I am what will keep you on your toes and always out of trouble
I am what will give you a concretial argument and an unbeatable rebuttal

I am what transforms the blindness of a man into clear sight
I am what will forever lead a person into the light

I am what comes with nothing but truth
I am what can always back it up with the hidden proof

I am what people put to the side for other worldly things
Instead I am what more people need to contain more inside their heads

I am what will give your thought process a whole new edge
I am what ones who do have it going on call knowledge

LAST CALL

We all have times in our life when we have to face a new crossroad
Which way we turn is crucial to our future and could flush down the commode

Sometimes things come in and turn your life around with no other choice
There are times when you must act as opposed to using your voice

I say that to say that I'm at my own crossroad, and the decision has been made
I know exactly what's in store for me
My debt has already been paid

I'm extremely thankful for what has come into my life, and I will cherish it forever
This is my time, my journey
It's now time to get it together

Lil' Duval helped get me in the mind-set of getting mine and living my best life
It's amazing when you've been blessed with a friend who is your future wife

Life is amazing and crazy with so many twists and turns
We have to learn from our countless scars and burns

The year 2018 was beyond a rollercoaster ride, and
I've learned many valuable lessons
Through all we go through in life, it's amazing to receive such blessings

I can't wait to usher in this new year
It's the return of the man for me
My future is so bright with happiness
I can hardly see

I'm so happy that I have this opportunity to be born
anew with my best friend by my side
Doing things in my olden days would be straight-up suicide

My time is now
I'm taking control
I'm owning it all
My only direction is up and up
I won't ever again fall

So if you're not with me and against me, for your sake, stay outta my life and my way
I have no room for crabs and haters
You have exceeded your stay
My destination is one that I've paid my dues toward,
and I will see it through to the end
Last call for the special few who are with me
Three, two, one . . . Begin

LIFE LESSON I

We all have our own life with a lot going on
Seems sometimes you're singing a brand-new song

A song that's gut-wrenching, surely to get you into tears
With the feeling of that one situation lasting for years

Life can be hurtful, difficult, and very hard to manage
Some do the ultimate because they just can't stand it

You try to go left but end up going right
It's like every step you take is a constant fight

We all have to keep our cool, stay positive, and strive for the best
Life is full of chaos, roadblocks, hurricanes, and many tests

Trying your damnest not to upset the one you're with
Time and love is much more valued than a simple gift

At the end of the day, valued time is all that is desired
But fighting for it constantly will drain and make you tired

We're all not perfect
Trust me, I have my own faults
Maybe this is karma at its finest, teaching what needs to be taught

We all can learn life lessons from each other
We're never by ourselves

At times, pride needs to be set aside
Reach out your hand and ask for help

LOVE

There's this thing in this world that we call love
This thing called love can take you down below and even high above

Now love is a very beautiful thing if you know how to handle it
If you're not sure what you're doing, you'll be knee deep in shit

Oh yes, I've had my share of love a few moments in time
A thing so beautiful, it will have you broke without even a dime

Love can be sweet and special and other times cast an evil spell
This is where you have to be careful or end up in hell

Now I'm not gone go into detail about my love past
I'm just trying to stick through today, trying to make my current love last

Life can be very hard, with so many trials and tests
I wanna master this art and have it down pat as opposed to just doing my best

There are some out there whom I've hurt dearly, turning their lives around
Hurting them was never the intent on my behalf
That's not how I get down

For those of you I hurt, I beg for your forgiveness
I honestly didn't mean it
I'm still learning for myself
For the casualty I'm sorry to have inflicted

Again, I have my own problems, and it's a struggle every day
Trust me when I say I'm doing the best I can to make tomorrow better than yesterday

There's also a point where you're straddling the fence, indecisive on which way to go
Do I stay?

Do I leave?
Do I wait?
Who in the hell knows?

When that comes in to play, I have to get on my knees and ask for guidance

I'm really stressing out
This whole love deal has me very tense

Love is supposed to feel good, with high feelings and free happiness
Help me, God,
I just want to be happy
Help me get off this fence

At the end of the day, I long for true love and its true definition
A true and solid love with one woman and no addition

Love, don't count me out
I'm still searching and gunning for you, love
Please don't ever give up on me because I won't ever give up on you

MESSED UP

Constant reminders and ongoing skepticisms, all these I stopped abruptly
The fact remains that through it all, I still messed up

Knowing what's right but still doing wrong and such
It still remains that, again, I messed up

I had plenty chances to stop it and keep that door shut
In the end, I still managed to once again mess up

I have no one else to blame, going on as not to give a what
At the end of the day, I still managed to mess up

Gotta look in the mirror
Face myself and family
This is deeper than any cut
When it all boils down, I'm ultimately the one who messed up

Gotta face reality and give it to God, praying for some kind of grace and luck
I hope that I can be forgiven by God and all for me messing up

Butterflies all in my stomach
I'm scared like a little pup
Simply because I got myself in another situation
where I again notoriously messed up

I'm gonna change my ways
Do the right thing and never ever again to mess up
I will be a new person with great strength and will
because this time I really fucked up

MIND WEALTH

I wanna write some positive words, words that have deep meaning
I want to put it on paper, ideas that'll make the blind see again

I wanna express my thoughts on an elevated level,
thoughts and words that will help excel

Excel the thought process of what we as humans have, giving words
of enlightenment and knowledge, not just a gift for gab
We all have our own way of thinking, some better than others
There are even some mindless people who will keep you running for cover

I want a better future for our existence, people using their third eyes
It's come to a point where all the pointless knowledge we must kiss goodbye

If you don't read or even hear my words, pick up a book and read for yourself
Take a look at the news and notice those around you—we truly need help

The mind is very mysterious and has many mystical ways
We must start using it to the fullest to ensure better days

Don't let everything be given to you
Research and know for yourself
I'm no preacher, just a servant, a servant promoting mind wealth

MY BRAIN

My brain is my weapon of choice
It feeds the words of when I open my mouth and use my voice

My brain is the very vital part of who I am
It lets many things inside as opposed to a dam

My skin is the largest organ, but my brain is the most powerful
It's the one thing that makes me more intriguing and wonderful

This is not a claim to say that I'm better than the next man
I'm only claiming that I constantly use it all day, filling and using it as much as I can

You see, my brain, I'm constantly feeding it knowledge
There are plenty of books out there, no necessary need for a school or college

Reading is fundamental, but I don't mind paying a fee
Price means nothing when it comes to helping this blind man see

Brain teasers and word games keep my mind sharp and on alert
When it comes to my brain, I don't mind putting in work

An educated person like myself is someone you should always be aware of
I don't have a college degree, but from what I've fed
my brain, my intellect is in the sky above

I write these words to share with you the importance of reading and research
There's so much to gain from it
It's very rewarding, and it doesn't hurt

There have been instances where I've been called into HR for this and that reason
But to see the look on the HR person's face when I
quoted their handbook was so very pleasing

As you can see, at all times, knowledge is always power
Let your brain keep you elevated, higher than any tower

Again, I don't need evil intent, weapons, or physical aggression to inflict pain
When I want to make my point or get ahead in life, I
use the greatest weapon of all, my brain

MY PLANET

I am my own planet, floating along in my own orbit
I am my own organism, my own world, with only a specific few that can fit

You see, I have my own weather, my own storms, and my planetary problems
At times, it seems that my solidarity is the only way to solve them

Trust me when I tell you, I have waves and winds
turning my planet into something fierce
I'm struggling every day, trying my best to topple this four-layered tier

Some may say I'm selfish in the way that I run my planet
The truth is, at times, there are instances where I can't even stand it

So as I rotate along, simmering in my own orbit
Be patient until I find a place for those who care to fit

I am a planet that is truly hurting inside, with so much pain and erupting volcanoes
With a priceless love that waits in the darkness that only a few really knows

I write these words to share my reason for my planetary actions
I write these words to show that with all my flaws, I do have a great passion

A passion for truth, understanding, and overall, an oceaning deep love
I pray for an equilibrium in my planet, radiating from the true God above

I have to say that my planet is full of vast green land, still and calm waters
A planet so beautiful, it can withstand anything, with way more to offer than others

My planet is currently under construction, so please mind the mess
Planet Surreal will be ready for that special spirit just as soon as I pass this test

MY SIMPLE PRAYER

I'm in a situation right now I'm frustrated and scared
I really don't know what to do
From my childhood raising and many thoughts and
praying, I simply have to turn to you

Though we're gonna make mistakes, some worse than
others, please, God, come take my hand
I wanna do the right thing and walk in your path, Lord
I'm doing the very best I can

God, I come to you now with a sincere and open heart,
begging and pleading for forgiveness
The lies, the cheats, those ungodly ways, and all my countless acts of selfishness
I ask that you take my hand and never let it go even when at times when I pull away
I pray this simple prayer that you guide my thoughts and actions each and every day

MY WORLD

Alone, constantly trapped inside my own little world, keeping
everyone out and letting none of my inner secrets unfurl

To me, this is the only way that I feel safe and secure
No one could ever get to me or ever hurt me, and this, I am sure

It's not that I don't want anybody in my head
Majority of the time, I'm the only person I can trust
My mind is my special space
Like a clubhouse keeping all the unwanted out is a must

Some may think it's mean, but anyone who knows me will say that I'm a nice guy
Yet always keeping them wondering, asking how, what, and why

To be quite honest, my own mother and brother doesn't know who I really am
For all they know, I'm one whom they love and who
gets my ways from my dad, Catfram

I really don't know what else to say
Everything that needed to has been said
Besides, if I say too much, some may get sneaky and attempt to enter my head

There's only one person who is in my world
If you know me, then you know who she is
She's the only one who will ever know my heartful, intimate, and sorrowful business

So if you ever see me sitting alone all to myself like a scared little girl
Just simply let me be
Let me chill out and relax in my own little world

NEO LESSONS TO TAKE YOU FAR

There are some in the world who possess the smarts and intellect of Albert Einstein
Though there are a few others who are not as fortunate and simply are one of a kind

There are some who are book smart at the same time lacking in other areas
There are some who have PhDs in life, but that A or
B grade in class is yet to be discovered

Then you have those others, you know, the ones who just know every damn thing
To try to inform or teach them something new, there's nothing to bring

I wonder where their wisdom comes from
Especially at a young age, I always thought wisdom and knowledge
are gained from experience, you know, living day to day

I've always been one to hang around older men and
women, getting a confirmable aspect on life
Attempting to have an exciting and peaceful life as opposed
to a hateful and dreadful one full of strife

I really feel sorry for them
My heart goes out to them
So much in life to watch out for, so many things that I can show them

I would never say that I know everything because
there's still much more for me to learn
I'd rather give my little wisdom away as opposed to it being earned

I originally entitled this piece "Smart Dumb Asses,"
but after writing, I had a change of heart
I'd rather have a more subtle and intellectual approach
simply titled "Neo Lessons to Take You Far"

RUNNING AWAY

Ever have that feeling of not knowing what to do in a
crowd full of people but still, there's only you?

Constantly trying to do the right thing, but it goes wrong every day
Searching long and hard, trying to find the correct way

Giving up has never been an option
I can't ever leave in defeat
Striving to get the wind beneath my wings and the ground beneath my feet
Is it bad luck, a bad hand, or am I just going about it all wrong?
One thing's for sure, I've been singing this sad song far too long

A complete turnaround is what I'm striving for, wishing and
praying hard that I finally open the correct door

Yes, I am very different from others
You can hear it in the words I say
Though different doesn't mean that I should be treated in a different way
I'm trying my best to catch up to the level where I wanna be
With my determination and God, that will all come to be

These words come straight from the heart, what I feel
What more can I say?
Though it crosses the mind and easy to do, I won't ever give in and run away

SINCERE

There are times in our life where we make some very bad choices and mistakes,
causing nothing but harm and hurt, looking at all the time you've wasted

I definitely have had my share of causing harm, pain, and too
much hurt, but knowing and completely understanding that
you are the cause of that pain is what hurts worse

Baby girl, I can't ever tell you how sorry I am for all the pain that I caused you
Sorry can't ever excuse nor void the actions I did toward you

I won't ever tell you to forget it, but I do beg of your forgiveness
I can publicly say I'm remorseful for my actions in front of a crowd of witnesses

So many things have come about in my life that have
really turned my thinking and life around
I've been doing so much to be a better man, constantly
moving up and never backing down

I seriously want you to know that I mean all these words that I speak to you
I wish and pray nothing but happiness, love, and success for you

I can't ever go back and change all the things that I've done
But all those things have helped mold me into the current man that I have become

I talked with my mom about the past and told her that
I'm not proud or happy for what I did
I also told her that that way of thinking is nonexistent, and I've gotten rid of it

My past and current prayers have constantly been for your true happiness in life
My prayers have been for a special man to treat you better than I ever did as his wife

If you don't ever speak to me again, trust, I fully understand and totally deserve it

This is the fate of my actions, actions that I have to live forever and deal with

The thing that brought me to telling you this is me owning
my actions and evolving as a better man
I hope that you can take all this in, know that I am sincere, and you understand

Again, this is my apology to you, and I wish and pray
nothing but the absolute best for you
I won't ever forgive myself, Tiffany
These words that I speak to you now are for once sincere and true

No more mess or stress
Continue to be blessed

TEMPTATIONS

Temptations, yes, that's the subject for this piece
Some of you now have a situation that's been going on for weeks

Don't you feel bad and don't you feel shame
Try to keep your cool, focus and maintain
Maintain on the positive and leave the bullshit behind
In life you must grow wiser
Never ever easy, it comes with time

There are some situations and tests that we habitually fail
Giving you a bad name and rap, with only horrid stories to tell

We must learn from our mistake s and resist the temptations
Everything is not good for you that gives you heavenly sensations

Of course it's easier said than done
The flesh can be something serious
Leaving you to a point where all you will call on is your God or Jesus

What I'm trying to say is don't let temptations get your back to the wall
In the end, leaving you all alone, by yourself, and nowhere else to fall

Keep a strong mind, a strong heart, a strong spirit, and a strong personality
Don't let your encounters with temptations result into your harsh reality

WHO CARES

So you got stuck with being overseas
Well, guess what, me too
Who cares?

You say this was your last semester before graduating college
Damn, you go to school for free
Who cares?

So you've never been away from home this long
You signed the contract
Who cares?

You can't have a drink because you're not of age
Another thing that comes with signing that contract
Who cares?

So you have to get all of your shots over again
At least you'll be healthy
Who cares?

You say you're not getting paid
Bah, damn, that sucks
Who cares?

So you have a sprained ankle
Hey, we only have three more miles
Who cares?

You're gonna miss your child being born
You get to see him when you get back
Who cares?

Your promotion warrant didn't come through
Don't worry
Be patient
Who cares?

So you don't have SAPI plates in your vest
You have faith in god, right?
Who cares?

You lying here breathless and lifeless
Now you'll never feel pain again
Who cares?

I care . . .
Who are you?

I am his mother
This is his wife, and this is his daughter

BECAUSE OF YOU

I'm in a real-life, new-age addition of Othello, and it isn't nowhere near good
I've been barred from seeing this wonderful woman
I've been totally misunderstood

In the case of Othello, he wasn't allowed to be with his love because he was a Moor
But because of my past marriage, I can't even get to the front door

Yes, my marriage wasn't the best, and truly I am the cause of it all
I also understand you don't want me to be your daughter's demise and downfall

I don't fault you for being a parent, but she is thirty years old
Let her be
Be honest—are my past actions of my previous marriage all that you see?

Just to let you in on a secret, I told your daughter all about it myself
Our relationship revolved around honesty and truth being dealt

She knows I wasn't the best husband and how I treated my wife
She knows how that's something that's forever stuck in me like a knife

She knows that when I say "I love you," I truly and honestly mean it
She knows that for her and her son, there's nothing I wouldn't do or get

It really pains me deeply to know that in your eyes,
I'm not good enough for your daughter
It saddens me that you forgot about forgiveness taught by our spiritual Father

Yes, I've made some bad mistakes, and I'm man enough to claim it yet move on
Is my past relationship gonna always be the broken song?

People do make mistakes, but some of us grow up and turn it all around
I'd never ever do your daughter the same as before
We have a solid ground

Not a day goes by that I sit and wonder what would
have come with the true connection we had
The fact of the matter is that other than me, it's your
own daughter who you've hurt and made sad

Ask her how she feels, and really listen with not only your ears but your heart
We may have lost the best thing that we found simply because you kept us apart

BITCH-ASS NIGGAS

Bitch-ass niggas, oh, I can't stand them
Ones who act like a girl or bitch as opposed to a guy or a him

Keep my name out your fucking mouth
You don't know me
Do that shit again and see if I don't make your mouth bleed

This is not a threat
I'm just giving it to you real
When it comes to bullshit, that's a game I don't deal.

In this world, there are too many critics and reporters
Because of people like you, some get missing or even tortured

You know so much about me, but I know nothing of you
Be a man and come to me so you can do an interview

I'm a grown man, and I don't have no time for games and bullshit
Step out of that bitch's attire and be a straight-up man for a bit
If you have something to say or questions, please come to me and say it
Just come to me real
Just please leave out the bullshit

I strongly advise you to listen and take heed to these words
When you come to me like a bitch-ass nigga, you are setting up your own curse

BULLSHIT 101

Some people like to play games and bullshit for political reasons or just for fun
But you can't bullshit a person who's mastered the art of bullshit 101
Playing head games and strategized moves, thinking that we're dumb

Please don't try and bullshit me
Trust me, I'm not the one
If you have something on your agenda, be a man and don't frontally lie to my
face and inform me with a bullshit excuse, trying to be deceptive and sneaky
Through all your deceptions and your fucked-up ways, I can see through it all

Take it from me
The bullshit that you give, it will be the reason that you fall

I can't fall for everything that you tell me
I was raised to have common sense
You cannot pull the wool over my eyes like Donald Trump and Michael Pence

You see, this puppet's creator and father has passed away,
so my strings have been cut some years ago
What you have in front of you now is not a boy but a man
giving it to you raw and real just so you know
There are many things that I am but a dummy I am not
Heed these words before you look stupid later on with your mouth poked out

At the end of the day, I demand respect and, damnit,
that's exactly what I'm gonna get
And all that shit that you said before, trust I didn't forget

Life and work can be so much smoother if you stopped acting like a bitch
Keep that shit up, and I'm telling you, you may wind up being found in a ditch

For your sake, you can't fuck with people's intelligence or, better yet, their mind

You can't play with the most prized possession I have
That's all mine

If I've hurt your little feelings by writing these words, then that says a lot about you
Maybe you need to switch your actions and some of the things you do

Just stop with the riddles, games, word configuration, and all the bullshit too
Remember karma's a cold bitch who's always on
her job just waiting to get back at you

DIFFERENT BUT ONE

With so much shit and chaos going on in the world
There are still biased people who makes me sick and hurl

There are too many different aspects of people
Some strange, some rare, and some are typical

The typical cold-hearted people who are quick to judge another
Judging another for their religion, sexual preference, or color

This form of profiling is painfully hard to bear
If there's someone different from any type, they have no kind of care

What really makes me sick are those who have been persecuted for their religion
To only turn around and do the exact same to others for whatever reason

I wanna know the reason why and how a person can be so mean and cruel
What justifies them being so hateful and spiteful, being a bigot and a fool

I just wish for once in this lifetime, that we would be a real human race
I'm praying for a world where there's no kind of racism or prejudice that takes place

The last time I checked, God gave man dominion over the animals and the earth
God is the only one who has dominion over man and responsible for our birth

DIFFERENT STROKES

We as a human race have many things about us that make us different
But the constant ridicule, anguish, and hate really makes no sense

In the animal world, all animals get along unless you're the prey
Sad that we as a people can't get it right for just one day

Skin color or ethnic background is the main culprit of the constant hate
Don't people realize that their life and soul are at stake?

Gender and sexual preference are another big people divider
Who am I to say he can't be with him and she can't be with her?

It goes even further to political party or even the state or area you live in
Even the stupid gangs killing over red, blue, or yellow have to jump in

I've seen families torn apart by a football rivalry
Truly a house divided
The sad part is that most of these ideas are taught when they are just young kids

We do have different aspects of the human race, but that just makes us unique
Yes, be proud of your uniqueness but not to where you place people under your feet

If the millions of species of animals can coexist, why
the hell can't we? Showing love is easy
It takes no real effort, and it's stress free

I do pray for a world where we all can love and get along
Then we shall overcome and fight
The power has been sung for far too long

So love someone else just as much as you love yourself
Go and hug someone that's different from you and try to love someone else

DON'T BE THE ONE

Who the fuck you think you're talking to like that?
Last I checked, 2005 was when my father passed

Think you all high and mighty with them stripes on your collar?
I don't give a fuck what your rank is
I'll crack your skull with a bottle

You need to get out of my face and you better do it quick
What the fuck you said, bitch?
Where's that damn brick?

You can talk to others that way
I personally don't give a shit, but don't think for one minute
You can bring that shit here, and your ass won't get hit

Respect you?
What the fuck you mean respect you?
I know you didn't go there
You got as much as respect that Samson had after Delilah cut off his hair

Why the fuck am I sitting here arguing with you?
Dog, what the fuck you wanna do?

Let me get out of here because this shit is pointless
Did you just touch me?
Damn, here comes the hit list

Ribs broken, arm broken, jaws wired shut too
Damn, what the hell done happened to you?

It's like what Surrency said when this deployment first begun
Watch your mouth, watch your ass, and please don't be the one

GOD BLESS THE CHILD

If these words are meant for you, then put these shoes on and wear it
If they're not meant for you, then make claim to these words and endorse it

I have a real big heart, but some of you take my kindness for weakness
I'm sick of this game you play
It's the time for a whole new season

No, I'm not being mean
I'm just being firm
It's past time you mofos sit back and learn

I work hard every day
Why don't you do the same?
Take care of your own self
It's simple and plain

Yeah, you have a situation, but really who doesn't?
I'm supposed to go broke for you because you are my cousin?

Family is great but sometimes it is a curse
Still owing me money all the way to your hearse

Yes, I'd do anything for you, and that's where I'm to blame, but
the constant handouts are causing me to go insane

It's not just family
Your friends can get you too
You know you have a bill to pay
It's your check that you blew

I don't understand the logic behind it, and I never can pay
all your bills late, but what about the surreal bill?

Oh yeah, that's right—you'll get me back next week
Hey, nice new Jordans that you have on your feet

Have some decency in you, and at the least consider my feelings
It's the same sad story with you
Who am I kidding?

Money doesn't grow on trees and definitely not on me
If it's really that bad, then it's God you should see

No, I'm not looking down at you
You had the same opportunity as me
I told you about that job and school
You chose not to inquire and see

Some have extreme circumstances, and trust we are kindred with each
other, but it's really past time for you to make something happen
Get up and make a hustle

Cash App is the worst
I curse the guy who created it
That app is the devil
It's made me so damn sick

If you're putting your hand out, simply leave me the hell alone
Remember, God blessed the child who has his own

GROWN-ASS BITCHES

Bitches, something I may never fully understand, those who
prefer to act like hoes as opposed to a grown man

Letting the smallest of things tick them off, showing
the proof of them being extremely soft

Wanna get all huffy and puffy and even roll their eyes
Come on, tell the truth
are you a female in disguise?

Some take it further and give the silent treatment
I swear this shit is way beyond my level of believement

It's amazing that they are deep down true punks
With the fucking nerve of parading around as the baddest of hunks

I don't know what their problem is, but they need to get it straight
I don't do good with assholes and bitches and especially those who are fake

All I'm saying is keep it real for a change
Stop flaunting around like you got a pussy stuck in your pants

You wanna act like a bitch, then I'll treat you as such
Here's a skirt, get on your knees, and don't forget to tuck

Some want to put it on the parents and say they're to blame
But the whole damn point is that it's a fucking shame

It's not that I don't respect them
Well, I really don't have to deal with them day to day
It is something I do not want

If I ever wanted an attitude from someone, I'd go home for that shit
But I'll be damned if I take it from a grown man that stands when he pisses

I've said it before, and I'll say it again
I don't know what their fucking deal is
May fate come to you and God be with you
To all you grown-ass bitches

I CAN'T STAND

So you want to know about my religious and spiritual belief?
I'm truly afraid you can't handle what comes out my mouth and through my teeth

Being that you've treated me like crap and had the gall to come at
me like this, well, you've earned everything I'm about to say
You're gonna get your wish

Yes, I have a spiritual belief
My mom planted that seed long ago simply because she loves me
As time goes by and going through life, there have
been several factors that affected me

The first thing that caught my attention was the miniseries *Roots*
This was my introduction into the mischievous world of religious cahoots

Yes, I said cahoots
We all know that the church isn't the most friendly and inviting place to be
Too many people in the church and the pulpit portray one life but live differently

Don't get me wrong—I totally understand the challenges
of trying to improve your life and soul
But you have to stay on one side of the fence, choose a side, and take control
Of your life

I'm tripping hard right now simply because you already
know I feel some type of way about the church
Then you come and prove me right about everything I've
been saying, making the situation even worse

I'm serious—this is crap
You point your nose down at me as if I'm just all around wrong on what I believe

Well, why are you portraying a Christian when that's
definitely not the idea of life you conceived?

I've been told by my bishop that the church is full of former this and that
From what I've been seeing, all those so-called past sins are a current act
I know I have my demons and temptations, but at
least I'm honest about it, no facade here
Yes, I am a struggling man, doing all I can to be a better man just so that we're clear

That's one of my biggest problems about the church, and this I mean you
preaching in the pulpit on Sunday but previously had a mistress all in-between

Please don't come at me with all that mess you have coming out of your mouth
Check yourself first and then, only then, you can look elsewhere and venture out

Even with all the shenanigans that are being portrayed, I
still stay all because of the feeling and love I get
I love you to life and I put that on my life, but how you
switched up on me and changed I can't ever forget

It's so funny how at the end of the day, it's us heathens who have
to teach church folk how to act and treat your fellow man
If you don't like what I just said, then change it for the better
simply because the crap you give, I cannot stand

JUDGE ACCORDINGLY

I was recently told something that made me feel some type of way
Leaving me stunned and speechless, I mean with nothing to say

I know we all have our opinions, no matter who you are
But this sort of stuff has gotten out of hand and gone too far

Before you pass judgment on someone, know who they are and what they're about
Know the real truth about them beforeyou shut them out

This especially goes for people who claim god and are busy in the church

With my dealings with Christians, they are the main ones who cause so much hurt

Oh yes, I have my faults, and I'm never ashamed to admit them
But I won't ever point a finger to someone else and condemn them
Last time I checked, everyone in the church is a former
this and former that, some still current
I could have sworn it's nothing to do whit what you want,
then ask for forgiveness and simply repent

Smile in my face, tell me you love me, and pray for me with the use of holy water
But have a total change of heart when you find out
I'm talking to your beloved daughter

In your eyes, all you see is two people dating, headed into some type of relation
The truth is all it's ever been is a good friendship and good conversation

I do understand you being motherly and wanting to protect your own
I also understand that it's easier not to get hurt when you're single and alone

I can't ever pass judgment on anyone
That's not who I am or care to be

So who are you to judge, set a stigma, and place judgment on me?

No, I'm not mad at this person
I'm simply just upset
I know I'm not worthy of this judgment to get

I've seen many friendships and relationships ruined because of this type of act
As a person and as a Christian, I do know that this is not how you're supposed to act

So before you point your finger, look down, and form an opinion against me
Take a look in the mirror and judge yourself and remember to judge accordingly

JUDGE NOT ME

Judge not, says the Lord
We have all come short of his glory
No matter who you are or what you are, we all have the same ole' story

Mistakes are gonna be made, some worse than others
Some leave us confused, upset while crying under the covers

On that same note, if I'm guilty of sin, how can I point a single finger?

I expect for you to do the same
If not, stay quiet and don't even hinder

It's funny how at times we forget about our hectic past
Knowing that you've done damage too with the spells that you have cast

It's hilarious that the people you've done dirt with
can open their mouth with judgment
Doing things we weren't supposed to do without even my wife's consent

I'm no angel myself, and I've always been man enough to admit it
God knows my heart and our conversations about
my ungodly ways I've been trying to kick

He knows about the conversations with my bishop and me opening up to other men
He knows how I'm not proud of my wrongdoings and the times I've stayed up crying

I'm not perfect
I have my faults, and I pray about them all the time
Again, who are you to judge me and sentence me for my crime?

We all need each other, but in the end, our journey is our own
If you don't have anything positive to say, then please leave me alone

If you know me, I've never pointed a finger because I do live in a glass home
No matter what you do in life, I'm gonna come at you in a loving and calm tone

Not once did you ever ask how I was feeling or ask about my concern
Instead you just scolded me and told me which way to turn

I'm truly at fault for what happened, and I'll lie in the bed I've made
I take everything you say with a grain of salt
Trust me, the message has been relayed

If you are my friend and truly want to help, then get on your knees and say a prayer
That's the best way you can show me that you do really care

I write these words to express my feelings about
something that's been bothering me
Just to be clear, there's a big difference between loving
and judging people, and that includes me

LEADERS AND FOLLOWERS

Got a brand-new job that can certainly pay every bill
With the location and perks
For this job, people would kill
To get ahead in this business, there is much there is to know
But if there is no training and poor guidance, how in the hell can you grow?

Being a low man on the totem pole, it's easy to see everything from the bottom up
From all the weight on my shoulders, it's clear to
know how bad things are fucked up

Do I have a voice?
Yet do I have an opinion?
Umm yeah, I have some big and great concerns
You would think the way shit's been hitting the fan lately
that they would shut up, listen, and learn
I would never say that I know everything, but I can tell when things are not right
Most of these things take common sense, are obvious, big as day in plain sight

If there's anyone they should be mad at, it's easy
Go in the bathroom and look in the mirror
No matter what you think or how big your title is, there is no one here who's inferior

If you understand physics or any corporation, you
would know that it falls from the top
It would be great if they could take responsibility and
stop portraying something they're not

The phrase "to be a leader, you have to be a follower" is a very,
very true statement and shouldn't be taken lightly
Just remember, at one point in life, the leader was a follower,
feeling down from work, talking to the Almighty

LESBIAN DILEMMA

This is some straight bullshit
I can't even slide in
Everywhere I look, dudes left out to women on women

I don't get it
This has got me fucking buzzed
Everywhere I look, women being with women just because

All I ever wanted to do was dance, nothing else
If I want to have a good time, I'd have to be a lesbian with bells

I'm seriously trying to understand this huge and crazy dilemma
I guess a strong back and a hard penis . . . hhmm, I can't ever give her

Opposites are supposed to attract and arouse the other on the POA
A man has to be sulibent or settle for another brother

That second part's not happening here
I love women too much
Still can't go to the crew bar without me saying, "What the fuck"

I'm not mad at anyone at all
Please do you and do what you do
I just wanna be able to enjoy myself and have fun with a woman too

This is not a complaint, just a mere observance and an honest concern
At the end of the day, there are many straight men here who a woman is all we yearn

LOVE ME OR HATE ME

Either love me or hate me, there's no in-betweenEither love me or hate me
Do I really have to say this twice?

Either love me or hate me
My patience is wearing thin, no time to be nice

I know there are things about me you don't like, but truly, it goes both ways

I strive for peace and serenity
You can't ever bring down my days

All the behind-the-back talking, yes, words do always get back to me
Though I'm not around all the time, I have many eyes that always see

See, the shit that you do is uncalled for
I don't do any of that to you

If you got a problem, you know the number
Be real
Be one hundred and keep it true

I want to be your friend and even closer than you could imagine

But at the rate you're going, this movie is over
Cut
That's a wrap
Fin

I know I'm not perfect
I have my own problems, but I can live with that
My biggest problem of all is when you act like an ass, always on the attack

I don't fuck with you
I leave you be
I strongly suggest you do the same

If you're ever worried about our relationship, hell, you're the one to blame

This could go so much smoother if you would do you and let me do me

Again, it's either you love me or hate me
Pick a side and let me be

LOVE-HATE FATE

This shit has my mind blown
I can't believe it's true
How can I still love someone the way I do even after the shit they do?

I'm always hearing how much she loves me and this and that
But honestly, no love has been ever shown
This is a sad fact

Words are a motherfucker and if not careful, they can fuck you royally
The proof is in the actions, showing the true meaning totally

Years and years have gone by when I've taken all her bullshit
Every time I think about it, I wanna throw up
It makes me so sick

I've done all I can for her, loving, caring, and even taking time out to spend with her
But every time she's in town, the thought of me is always absent and a blur

I've taken all that I can take, and as much as I don't want to, I must move on
I'm tired of this broken record player playing the same tired and sad song

I do really, really, really love her, and I feel stupid for feeling this way
But I'll be damned if I continue to take her bullshit coming my way

I never understood how you can say how much you love
someone but they can't ever, ever show it
I guess the proof of the pudding is that they never loved not one bit

I mean how do you come into town twice and never
have time to see the one you love?
Let me know when she comes into town who she's really thinking of

Now I'm not gonna point fingers and insinuate, but we both know the truth
So busy with God knows who, I can't even get a call from a phone booth

Even had the nerve to go back to my town after I've left the country
Again, I see what level I'm on when it comes to priority

Who am I kidding?
I don't ever see her ever really loving me that way
Chances are slim
I have a better chance of joining the KKK

It's so true that it's a thin line between love and hate
I do love and hate her all in the same breath
I guess with her that's just my fate

MAINTAIN YOUR OWN YARD

Some people can't mind their own fucking business
I'm sick of that game
Just worry about your damn self
It's simple and plain

Man, stay out of my life and keep your ass outta my yard
Wonder why you're fucked up because you played that card

I don't fuck with nobody, so don't fuck with me
They'll find your ass buried or hanging from a tree

I worry about myself
I can give a damn about you
Now who gave you the right to do the shit that you do?

Talking about we're brothers
Well I guess I'm a stepbrother
You acting like you found me on top of your mother

Thought we were cool, but to be honest, I'm not surprised I
dug deep in your soul when I first looked in your eyes

I put nothing past no one
The people I'm around is straight cutthroat
You better watch your ways, boy, or you will have a cut throat

I'm not a violent person
I'm as loving as they come
But because of your bullshit, I'll send you to Kingston kingdom come

Now all this would never happen if you just stayed in your lane
You'd be walking on sunshine instead of walking in pain

Again, this isn't my nature
I was truly born to love, so respect my reaction to your negative shove

Just mind your own business is all I'm saying
To keep from knocking you out, I'm doing overtime praying

So worry about yourself and maintain your own yard
Be a real fucking man and stop playing a facade

OH WHY

Once a whore always a whore
Sadly that's been the way I've been having to feel
No matter the changes and the difference, this is the fate of this deal

Yes, I've had some rollercoaster relationships—who hasn't?
But remember this one thing
All that is past tense

I've made some very bad decisions in my life
If possible, I'd take them all back, but why do people
constantly use my past ass the ammo for my attack?

My bishop always says that there are a lot of former this and that in the church
But for me not to get forgiveness and a second chance is what hurts worse

The real sad and ugly part is that I'm in love with an
incredible woman whom I cannot have
I mean not given the slightest chance to create our own future and our own path

Really, am I really that horrible of a person to the point where
I'm never good enough for a certain woman?
Why am I being ostracized, cast out, put in a corner, dammed, and condemned?

I swear all I ever wanted to ever do was truly, truly, and truly love this great queen
I'm sick of being treated like such a horrible guy who's wicked and obscene

This is a raw and ugly hand that I've been dealt, and the house is counting the cards
No matter what people say or think, I will always love
that woman, and without her, I'm lost

OUT OF MINE

I'm so mad right now
Like Tyson, I can bite a person's ear off
People all in my business, spreading lies and chaos
It's really got me pissed off

I don't mess with nobody
I keep to myself and mind my own business
The stuff I've had to go through lately is well past dumb and makes no sense

I really wish they will act their own age and truly grow the hell up
I'm a grown-ass man
Those days are over
This high school crap, man, I've had enough

If you got it on your chest, please be a man, grab a pair, and step up
If you're too much of a coward to say how you feel, grab
some milk, sit down, and shut the fuck up

People having a horrible life and can't stand to see someone else being happy
Constantly throwing salt in the other's direction,
trying to pull them down, being all crabby

I wish they can get their shit together and leave my name out of their mouth
I'm a real cool cat but, once you cross that line, that
whole coolness quickly goes south

I'm really not a violent person
I'm a true lover as opposed to a backyard street fighter
But don't think for one minute that I won't get stupid and set your dumb ass on fire

I'm gonna ask you nice, and I will be polite, but I'm gonna ask it only one damn time
I gotta a penny here for you to buy some business
and please stay the hell out of mine

PLAYING YOUR GAME

To all the women out there, know that I truly do love you
But I Can't get over some of the games that you play and do

Now I know we men have our faults and our bullshit too
But these words here are directed to the women who bullshit too

If you already know there's no chance between us, why play like it is
This is real life you're playing with, no Hollywood or showbiz

Giving me mad play as if our situation will go to the next level
You're playing with fire
All men are not the same
Please be careful

If there's no other level, then keep it on the ground floor
Let me know up front that there won't be anything more

Also, if you know that I'm attached to someone
else, why the fuck did you tell me that
Knowing damn well there won't be nothing going on?
See, that's where that bullshit is at

Gonna tell me all your spots and what makes you squirm
Baby, I gotta go
This meeting is adjourned

Why I need to know about your special piercings and private tattoos
I can't know for myself
Not going that way
Stop leaving me fucked and confused

Want me to come over to chill out?
Oh, I meant really just cuddle, without having your ass all on me
I know you feel me poking you in the back
Yeah, that's real meat, and I don't have to pee

I'm too old for a sleepover
Believe me, girl, those days are over and done
I will always be your friend, and that's real talk, but a gay friend I'm not that one

For some damn reason, women always tend to say the
opposite of what they want and who they really are
I've been playing and winning your own damn game for a long damn time
This is when you get out of my car

So please don't play with my head and my other head, too, baby
That's just all around bad juju

For your own damn good, watch what you do and who you
do it with because it just may backfire on you

REAP WHAT YOU SOW

With all that sniggling and smirking, if you can see, it gets you nowhere
Couldn't you tell by my actions that I'm above it all and really don't care?

I really thought we were better than this
Isn't this supposed to be a family affair?
I guess that's what families do, leaving you out to dry with your ass in the air

What hurts me the most is that I thought we bonded and spiritually connected
I *over*stand clearly
Through everything I've tried and done, I was habitually
rejected

I seriously wanna know what is it that I personally did wrong to you
You talk about all my indiscretions, but what about all the shit that you do?

I've never been the one to go tit for tat, but let's even up the playing field
You're like Trump in the White House
Because of your name, you can do whatever you will

Now we both know that's wrong, but you gotta pay for your own sins
That's between you and God
So who are you to pass judgment on me and to come striking me with a rod?

All I ever, ever, ever wanted to do is love on you,
and in return, I thought I'd get it back
Instead, all I get is ass a kiss and a nose to look up at
What's up with all the that?

If you wanna check someone, do me a favor and please look into a mirror
Take a real deep look, and leave everyone else out
I promise it will become clearer

Your own dad said and proclaimed to keep your mouth off of God's children
Trust God has been good to me
I'm not stressing
Please don't miss your blessing

With everything you've been taught by your elders,
you're past the stage of being able to grow
A fact that we all know so well but it's obvious you forgot
Despite all things, you're gonna reap what you sow

RELEASE AND LET GO

This life we live, we all have our own choices and decisions
Some that leads into a life of happiness and others to some bad convictions

This life is what me make it
No matter what, it's our decision
It is our own decision, our own thoughts with our own vision

Of course we do not know everything in this life, and at times, we need a hand
But don't get upset with me when I don't wanna choose your plan

I really appreciate your words
Deep inside, I know that you mean well

At the end of the day, this is my life, my road, my own tale

The autobiography that I'm writing can be and will be only written by me
My life will end with a very happy ending
Just sit back, watch, and see

Regardless of what you think, I am very happy with the choices that I've made
I just wish that you can be happy because I am happy
Did you hear what I said?

No, I'm not perfect, and of course I've made some mistakes
But you telling me what I'm not going to do is time and breath that's a waste

I've seen families torn apart, children stressed out
just because of someone else's opinion
Don't put that burden on your family please
You need to make the right decision

At the end of the day, it really isn't fair
You have to let people live their own life

Give them a chance to fly or fall
Take off the leash
Don't be in them like a knife

One day I'll have kids and I will always be there for them to assist them on their way
But I will be fair
Holding, not controlling, knowing that they are able
to have complete control over their day

With how some are treated by their family, the pain hurt
You can't fathom or know
It gets to a point where you really need to release and let them go

REMEMBER THIS

I'm tired of being restrained and restricted to the bottom of the pack
Got me scurrying for crumbs to eat just like a nasty lil' rat

No matter what I say or do, I cannot climb the ladder
Got my mind twisted, so instead of worse, I'm getting badder

Don't know who to trust or what to believe
Like a vulnerable baby, so easy to deceive

Why can't I get my forty acres?
I am far from being a tool

I'm majestic like a Clydesdale
I'm far from a mule

This is not living and I'm man enough to say it
God has my back
Give me a try, and you better bring it

I'm more than you think, and honestly, I'm more than you
I'm speaking from great experience
Take heed of these words which all are true

Test me
I'll pass it
Try me
I'll surpass it
Give me the job
I'll take over it
Give me the blueprints
I'll own it

Why must I be confined to such a murky and bottomless depth?
Are you afraid of what I can achieve?
This I know you can't accept

Try to uplift people at times as opposed to keeping them under your feet
The strings that you're pulling are more bitter than sweet

I know that you're on top with the power of running your own kingdom
Just remember the very spot to lead from can also be the same spot you hang from

RULES, REGULATIONS, AND BULLSHIT

In my lifetime, I've been subjected to many different rules and regulations
I've seen people punished for this and that, including executions

I understand the meaning behind having them in place

But some rules are total bullshit and should be exempted and also erased

Dealing with rules from grade school all the way to the Marine Corps
But it was the rules and consequences from my parents that made my ass sore

I know and understand rules are put into place to keep order and control
But there are some instances where rules are for those
who live on being a constant asshole

I'm sure you've seen it for yourself at some point in time
A person who has authority turning everything you do into a crime
I've worked for some companies where you couldn't even walk the wrong way
supervisors and so-called officers can't wait to fuck up your day

I'm not pointing any fingers or elbows, but you out there know what I'm talking about
Some taking you out of your character to screaming and cursing a whole other route

Some rules that are in place are crazy as hell and makes
no type of sense, keeping you on the defense
Walking a tight rope, trying not to catch a bad consequence
It's funny how some supervisors forget where they
came from or forget being at the bottom
Constantly keeping you in a frigid winter as opposed to a beautiful autumn

Again, I'm not against or opposed to abiding by the rules laid out
It's a matter of respect
That's all I'm really talking about
Treat people with dignity and some kind of respect
Remember, what you give out is also what you get

It's one point I'm trying to get across
Let it stick and don't ever forget there's a big difference
between rules, regulations, and bullshit

STAY THE HELL OUT OF MINE

Why you so worried about me?
You need to stay in your own yard
Stay the hell out my hand, man
Play your own card

My business is my business and neve r your concern
Get close to my flame, and I promise you'll get burned

This is no threat
It's a solemn promise
Send your soul away to heaven simultaneously with a forehead kiss

No, I'm not violent, but please heed the warning
I would rather give you love that's warm and charming
Life is so sweeter when you stay to yourself and concern your own,
so keep your opinions to yourself and leave me the hell alone

This is how I treat you and others, so please do the same
I speak English just like you, so my words are simple and plain

The world would be a better place if everyone thought the same as me
I care for you, man, but it's your life, not mine
I'm gonna let you be

Again, mind your own business
Stay out of mine
Next time, I won't be too kind
Just keep doing you because I'm de finitely doing
me, and please stay the hell out mine

TESTING

Tests, one of the aspects of life that gives it that extra spice
Some are minute and easy
Others are gruesome and not
Quite as nice

Tests are designed to measure the amount of struggle a person can handle
Not to infuriate people and have them burn up like a candle

Always hearing, be calm
It's all right
This is just a test but can never pass and win even when
they've done greatly and done their best

I truly believe others test you to only hold and keep you down
With no regard of how bad you feel and how much you frown

Why do some people test others, constantly putting them on the spot?
Always trying to place themselves in a position they're not in?

My face with bullshit I won't begin to tolerate
Giving birth to a sinful mind and feelings of hate

These feelings are deeply true, and you are the creator
Can't blame no one else but yourself for being found washed to the shore

That might have sounded a lil' drastic, but believe me, it can happen
Don't be the cause of your mother's mourning and sadness

Think
All of this can be prevented if you simply stay out of my face
Minding your own damn business and staying in your place

I never have anything personal against anyone, not even you
I thought you should know what testing me could lead up to

A MARINER'S LIFE FOR ME

I'm staring at the water
Stuck in its beautiful chaos
While taking out the trash, one look and then I was lost

Its beautiful splash and violent waves have gotten
me mesmerized and completely taken in
Been loving water my whole life, all I wanna do is dive on in

It's true to say that I can sit and watch the water all day long
Sending me to another place, another world, with a brand-new song

I'm connected to the water in a way I cannot explain
If I jump in this water, I may get fired, fired for being dumb and insane

On the other hand, I probably won't make it, having the water get the best of me
Swallowing me whole, doing a quick 180, going from my love to my worst enemy

I write these words to express my respect and love for this great ocean
I guess you can say it has a hex on me with its magic motion potion

I can write all day about the beauty of this water
This is something that everyone should see

I love my job and the beauty I get to see
Not a pirate but a mariner's life for me

BATHROOM CRISIS

Trapped inside the toilet, don't know what to do
Originally came in to pee but ended up having to do number two

How could this come so unexpectedly, so abruptly, and out of the blue?
Messing up all my plans, interrupting what I originally came to do

Can't be in here too long
She will wonder what is the matter
Gotta do something quick
Or have this meeting end up a disaster

Better get it done quickly and get it out the way
If she finds out what's happening, that'll be the end
Of my stay

I've done what I needed to do badly, but there is another issue
I've looked all over her bathroom only to find not one roll of tissue
What woman has no tissue?
How in the hell could that be?
Guess I have to use this white towel hanging with the name *Versace*

I'm glad I have matches
Good she has some spray as well
I have to camouflage this scent so there's no way she can tell

Well, I'm done with my business, and I've cleaned myself up too
Just in time because I hear her banging on the door to use the bathroom too

BATHROOM NIGHTMARE

Here I am trembling, shaking, and sweating, sitting on this porcelain throne
Wishing that I should have eaten something else
instead and left those hot wings alone

Devil's Breath sauce was the flavor I chose
I can't even tell you why
I guess it was the pretty woman in the tight red dress winking at me with her eye

I'm not even kidding you
I really am shaking and sweating
And that's no BS

Please, somebody call 911
There's a man in the bathroom who's in great distress

Oh my god, it hurts
Oooohh, it really burns
Please stay away from the door
This isn't your concern

I can hardly sit straight
I'm moving all over this toilet seat
I need more room to move around
Gotta get these pants down past my feet

I finally understand what it's like for a woman to be in labor and giving birth
Those wings were really good, but for all this, it's not even worth it

I need some bleach, a lot of water, and liquid plumber
I really have made a big mess
Don't you judge me
We've all had a shitty day

You know what, stay out of my business

Oooohhh, what a relief
I'm finished
I've cast that wet and nasty demon out of me
Now I'm in the shower, feeling great,
Oh damn, with all that going on at the time, I didn't have to pee

Now come on now, let's not point fingers
Who hasn't been in the shower and suddenly had to pee?
It goes down the drain with the rest of the water,
Everybody's guilty of this, not just me

Now I'm about to go to sleep
I'm cleaned and dressed
Lights off and about to say a prayer

Oh no, I jump out the bed and run to the bathroom for
another round of this bathroom nightmare

FOURTEEN WONDERS

I recently had the privilege of being a part of the best band in the land
If ever given the chance, I'd quickly do it all over again

A lot of times, I watch old tapes, listen to CDs,
reminisce and just let my mind wander
The ones I will cherish forever are the members of the Sounds of Thunder

What can I say about them?
Hell, I don't even know where to start
I know the thirteen who came up with me will forever be in my heart

Spread across from Miami to Detroit and even Houston, we all
met in Tallahassee in the fall of nineteen ninety-nine
Everyone having the same intention but the thought of our
newly founded bond never once came to mind

We've been through hell and back together, and this is most certainly the truth
IF they ever needed me for anything, there's nothing I wouldn't do

Yeah, we had our arguments and disagreements that could have led into a fight
But it was all good because we'd be drinking King Cobra together later that night

My place is your place—that's what we were all about
No matter what the situation, no one was ever left ass out
We most definitely had a lot of good times
A lot of times, I think back, laugh, and smile
Time flies by
Damn, I miss those cats
I haven't seen them in a while

Some have their own families and brand-new careers, but that is a part of life
Hell, I'm in the Marine Corps serving in Africa, away from my beautiful wife

No matter where we are, we will always stay in contact all the way to the very end
Those special thirteen are not only in my heart and mind,
but they have been engraved in my skin

I will always have love for the Hundred and of course the Sounds of Thunder
But there's no greater love than my love for the Fourteen Wonders

IS IT REALLY TABOO

I wanna discuss a certain subject that's frowned upon and considered to be taboo
Before you judge me sideways, I'm sure that at some
time in your life, you've thought of this too

We're attracted to who we're attracted to
There's no way getting around that
Some are attracted to the big, the small, the smart, the thug, the white, and the black

With all the huge LBGT campaign that's sparked
the nation, on a platform for all to see
Am I wrong if I'm attracted to certain people that's in my own family?

Now that question is rhetorical
No need to bite my head off or feel a certain way
I really don't need your permission or your going-to-hell sermon coming my way
I'm just being honest
The ones in my family are the products of some very nice genes
To say that I have an unattractive family is a lie and totally just obscene
I'm just stating the facts that no matter who they
are, we are human and living creatures
If that person is beautiful, sexy, intelligent, or fine,
how can you deny those features?

Sounds crazy to say, I can't even look at her like that because she's my family
I'm not even taking it there
I'm not going left
Be honest with yourself
Don't deny what you truly see

"Damn, if she wasn't my cousin" is a phrase that we all
have heard or said at some point in time
To act upon that thought is one thing, but to think it is natural and human

It is not a crime
I can't say personally, but I do know there are some who
have crossed that line to be totally honest with you
In most dynasties, that's something that's done all the time

You see, it's not taboo to everyone, only to certain cultures, religions, and cliques
If you travel to certain countries in the world, the thought
of it being taboo is quickly dismissed

of course, I've thought of it myself
Yes, that's my whole reason for writing this
Let a spade be a spade, and be honest with yourself
If they got it going, then that's just what it is

LOVE SONG

I'm so tired of being alone
This life isn't for me
I'm hoping to have that special woman to have our *anniversary*

I've been *searching* for those *better days*
Soon I'll have *my lady* just so I can give her *a million ways*

For the current moment, *I'm a mess*
I'm constantly searching out for true *love and happiness*

I hope I don't have to wait the *next lifetime* in order to find her
Wherever she is, I hope she's sweet as *brown sugar*

She must be a *special lady* and a very exciting girl
I'm hoping she *knocks my socks off* and also *rocks my world*

She will be *forever mine* and the *lady in my life*
I will always be *giving you the best that I got* to keep you as my wife

No matter what anyone says, *baby, I'm for real,* and *I choose you*
We will forever be together simply because *I put a spell on you*

Although she is *my angel* from above, *heaven can wait*
She has me *riding on a cloud*
The day she *meets me at the altar,* I won't be late

Her heart will always say, "*He loves me*" and "*Come inside, my love*"
This is a *sweet love*
I can't help it
I'm in love

MY FRANKENSTEIN WOMAN

I wanna play Frankenstein and create the perfect woman
Not with actual body parts but special features and such, you understand

I would start with the eyes of Phylicia Rashard, my, my, my
Eyes that hypnotize, trapping me in time as she passes me by

I have to have the lips of Adelle Givens, oh, so big and sweet
Making me want to lick her lips even right after she eats

But her smile and giggle will be that of Loretta Devine
A smile so beautiful and tantalizing, brightening any dark area at any time
Having the breast of Pam Grier, the name speaks for itself
To keep up with her, I'd be on a strict diet and ensure perfect health

With the cover girl hips of Queen Latifah, oh my damn
Giving me so much more to bite on than any turkey or ham

Her legs and thighs will be that of Serena Williams, didn't you know?
Something strong and powerful to lock me into place, with nowhere to go

Now what's a woman without a brain?
This is where Madam CJ Walker comes into play
Having intellect and smarts to ensure a prosperous and financial day

I'd have to pick my momma, for a woman is nothing without a loving heart
Always loving me back into position, always in my
corner no matter what, never ever to part

Like Lupita Nyong'o, her skin will be covered and wrapped in chocolate
Better than any candy or sweet, a taste so mouth-watering,
savored forever that you can't ever forget

So these are my special ingredients to create my special treasure
Keeping me happy for days and days with much love and of course much pleasure

I can't and won't lend her out to anyone
She will be forever all mine
Just thought I'd share with you the creation of my perfect woman Frankenstein

THE HUNDRED WAYS
Sounds of Thunder
Fall '99

You're at the battle of the bands or a simple HBCU football game
Though you've been to many before, there's something
about this one that isn't quite the same

Everyone's in suspense because they know what's about to happen
With the rolling in of eight charter buses starts the
stir of screams, yells, and clapping

Only one band is known to need the use of eight buses to
get them to where they're requested and wanted
I'm speaking solely of the world-renowned, incomparable
Florida A&M University Marching 100

Known for their innovations, precision drills,
formations, and crowd-spellbinding shows
Is the band coming
What will the hundred do next?
The suspense steadily grows

They start you off with their slow "One-Death March," a preview of what's to come
Along with the mystical voice of Joe Bullard and the
boom of the percussion scotch drum

They then rattle onto the field, marching 360 steps a minute
Their creativity stays fresh
They don't need motorcycles, fireworks, or gimmicks

When that sound hits your body, you then know that they are the absolute real deal
With the sound of Twentieth Century Fox giving
you hair-raising and goosebumps feel

There are some great bands out there, but the Hundred
wrote the syllabus and broke the mold
With a composer by the name of Lindsey B. Sarjeant
who writes with a pen of genius and gold

Their sound is unique and distinctive
It's a sound greatly powerful than any other band you've heard
Combining the use of fortissimo, tone, articulation, and
push-out instilled by their mighty professor

This is all due to the endlessly hard work of the late and great Dr. William P. Foster
.   His legacy continues on, and with that legacy, all
members continue to follow and look after

The most imitated band in the world, responsible for
numerous innovations, and that is indeed a fact
Band pageantry by William P. Foster, every band
director's syllabus is where this book is at

Professor Bing, Dr. Shaylor James, Longineu Parsons, Dr. Julian
White, and Dr. Shelby Chipman were some of the main tools
These are many of the great people who helped keep the mold of the Hundred's
core and values

Adored by many and praised by the thousands, plenty high
schools and colleges give the Hundred their due respect
The performances of the hundred imprinted in your memory
has always had a vast and rippling effect

The only HBCU band to be the recipient of the Sudler Trophy award,
giving all other bands something to strive for and reach toward

60 Minutes, Super Bowl performances, presidential inaugurations,
the Rose Bowl parade, and also the Grammys as well
The sole band from America represented in Paris, celebrating their
Bastille celebration, another accolade for the Hundred to tell

Their work is nonstop, practicing and performing all year

They literally work around the clock
You can hear the chants of "This Is a Hundred Show," "Take
Them to the Showers," and of course "Hubba Doc"

Qualities to live by to guide our thoughts and to rule our
actions/lives is the motto of the Hundred
If you never had the chance to see them in person, I urge you to check them out
To verify everything that I said

So do what you wanna
Sing, sing, sing
A tribute to Bob Marley, send out an SOS, and don't
forget the hay in storm and sunshine
No need for any black and blues
Just say, "La la," enjoy the good times, and have an oh happy day

THE PORN STASH

This piece is for the ladies
Because I want you to understand
This is my own version of Steve Harvey's *Think Like a Man*

There's one vital thing that's important to a man
This thing starts from boyhood continuing on to manhood

It has been said that we men think with our dicks and that's somewhat, kinda true
That's not to say we think with it on everything that we do

We men are naturally attracted to women
That's just the way we were built
So when you find porn in the DVD player, don't get mad and start pushing guilt

It's not to say we love you less
Sometimes you need to release and unwind
It's perfectly natural
Men and women have been doing this since the beginning of time

We men are different from women
Unlike women, we need a visual
Women, you do the same thing too, playing with yourself but only using your mental

Yes, I said it
There are plenty of you out there who has a dildo tucked away
Both men and women spend time with themselves for some self-on-self play

No matter the age, mostly all us men has a stash hidden
somewhere to quench that manly thirst
Remember, that's only for self-gratification
Women, you will always come first

So, ladies, don't get mad when you find out about his porn stash
Just be happy he's at home getting it on as opposed to tricking with cash

Let me tell it
Porn has saved plenty of marriages over the years
It beats spending all the bill money on a stripper or a hooker, leaving you in tears

So I hope you understand what it's like for a guy when
we sweat and start getting that urge
I'm giving it to you straight from a man's point of view
Please understand every word

So buy a flick or two and give it as a gift
You'll be amazed at what that will do
There are plenty couples who watch it together, creating
a new fun world and role-playing too

If used the right way, porn can be very instrumental in
your relationship and your bedroom too
Releasing stress and pressure, giving you both excitement
and also saving your relationship too